From a Corner of Comfort to a Land of CHAOS

J. R. Slade

From a Corner of Comfort to a Land of Chaos
Published through Hilltop Publishing

ISBN: 978-0-578-53184-7

Dedication

For my son Jamie who stepped up and took over many of my everyday chores during my absence, and my daughter Annika, who continued her steadfast commitment to her education without interruption.

Author's Note

The seeds for this book were planted when I started keeping a journal of my day to day actions while I was deployed to Iraq. They started to grow as I began writing for therapy.

Throughout the pages of this book, I attempt to share with the reader my unforeseen experiences while in Iraq. I write about my deployment to Iraq to participate in the "Operation Iraqi Freedom" (OIF) campaign, in 2006 and 2007. To avoid conflict or cause harm to anyone, most of the characters names were changed. I did not use the official name of the Iraqi military training school for similar reasons.

Not deliberately done, but the descriptions, locations, and incidents may not be exact, however, I did attempt to be as accurate as my memory enabled me to be. My reports, as well as my descriptions of violence, death, and corruption, were mainly taken from public media, such as CNN, British Broadcasting radio network, (BBC) and by word of mouth from my command, and the many conversations with my interpreters. The Iraqi soldiers who I worked with throughout my deployment also informed me on numerous incidents as well.

In writing this book I was forced to reckon with the sacrifices of being deployed. I learned to cope with life, death, and chaos. I now have a better understanding; knowing that there are specific reasons for each.

To this very day, I am grateful to God, for my survival, and for enabling me to write this book. In doing so, I vow to never forget the men and women who were also deployed on the mission but did not return.

1

It was almost sunset and I had just finished tying up my last bag of yard waste when I heard the squealing brakes of a large vehicle. It was one of those shiny brown UPS trucks, pulling up to the curb of my home. The driver exited his vehicle wearing his well-pressed brown uniform. I remember the driver approaching me with his eyebrows raised, and smiling. As he extended his arm to hand me the large envelope, he said, "I think this is important. I delivered several of these this week."

When the truck pulled away, I took a seat on the porch to open it. The envelope contained several copies of familiar documents. I read the papers numerous times. The documents were orders, from the Department of the Army. The orders read, "Temporary change of station in support of Operation Iraqi Freedom and return to Permanent Duty Station." I only remember it being a Monday, back, in March 2006. That was the day when a series of changes began to take place in my life.

Right from the beginning, I thought a mistake had been made. They contacted the wrong person, these orders are not for me, I said to myself. I felt that someone should have caught the error before sending the directives out to me, and getting me all worked up. I was wrong, it turned out the orders were indeed meant for me. The social security number on the papers were mine.

My hopes for retirement were unexpectedly dashed. I found myself at the core of a dilemma and was faced with a

1

no-win situation. The first challenge was breaking the news to my family. I didn't want to go into the house, because I did not know how to break the news to my wife, (Thekla) about the contents of the envelope. When I finally got the nerve to go inside, I concealed the envelope to avoid anyone from seeing it. I needed more time before breaking the news to my family.

It all was overwhelming, and so much to do, with so little time to do it. I waited until after dinner to tell my family the news. I needed extra time to search for the right words. As usual, the four of us gathered around the table for dinner. Thekla, my son (Jamie), my daughter (Annika), and myself. It was a typical evening at the dinner table. The three of them were laughing about a close friend who stopped by to drop off some freshly baked bread a few hours earlier.

Jamie was 24, already a few years into adulthood. He was working and studying at the local university. Annika was 17 years old, and we were looking forward to her graduating from high school in May. It was the month that I was deploying to Iraq after I completed my training. I interrupted their laughter and broke the news of my deployment, changing the mood from laughter to a somber one.

"There was some real serious news delivered to me today. News that concerns all of us," I said. "I received orders from the Department of the Army notifying me that I was chosen to be sent to Iraq, in a few weeks."

"Certainly not you!" Thekla said. "Look at you, you are almost 50 years old, and you're not in the best physical condition either. Besides, what makes you think that they will choose you?" The children thought it was all a joke. They too didn't believe a word of the conversation. "No, they're not," my daughter Annika said as if we were having just another normal family conversation.

My family had to mull over the news for a couple of days before it sunk in. I received more documents with further instructions in the mail, confirming what I already knew. The additional documents were more convincing to my family. They began to accept the reality.

The orders arrived at a time when I was months away from my 50th birthday. All along I had been thinking that I was getting a little too old for combat deployment. I had spent months telling myself it wouldn't happen to me because of two specific reasons; age and I was nearing the end of my career. Neither turned out to be a factor.

The war had been ongoing since 2002, and the thought of being deployed was always in the back of my mind. However, never did I think it would actually happen. Occasionally the commander would bring up the possibility of the unit as a whole being deployed during meetings. But, no one thought that individual soldiers would be selected.

As I neared the end of my 20-year military career, like many before me, I devoted a lot of time planning for retirement. In any case, I only had nine months left on my enlistment contract. I was really looking forward to my future. Along with that, the required physical challenges that had been implemented into the army's fitness program were becoming more strenuous on my body.

The deployment was for 15 months or longer, which meant there wasn't enough time left on my contract. I was not aware of an army policy concerning age and deployment at the time. Apparently, the army saw it differently. For the good of the army, my contract could be adjusted as needed, to meet their pressing demands. This is precisely what happened in my situation. I was a career soldier who had sworn to obey the orders of the President and the officers appointed over me. My deployment was one of those orders, and another was always be prepared, as well as staying physically fit.

A lot of transformations that affected my life took place all in one evening. As a family, we needed to come up with a plan for the future, during the time that I would be away.

Next, there was my day job. It was important that I inform my supervisor about my deployment notification quickly for two reasons. One was to be assured that I would have a job when I return, and two, it would allow them enough time to choose someone to work my position temporarily.

Just days earlier it was unthinkable, that I would be leaving the comforts of my home, and to be on my way to Ft. Mc-Coy Wisconsin, to begin training for war in Iraq. I had never heard of Ft. McCoy, so I started to do research. I emailed other soldiers I knew to see if they ever heard of Ft. McCoy. They had not.

I thought about the number of younger soldiers in the Battalion who could have been chosen other than me. Typically, a military Battalion is made up of 300 to 800 soldiers. In my reserve unit, the number was more like 125 soldiers, if that. Many of them often talked about volunteering to go to Iraq. However, for some unknown reason, I was the one chosen. When the younger soldiers heard the news that I was being deployed, some volunteered to take my place. Despite their efforts, they were denied the opportunity.

I had no choice but to confront the circumstances as they were. There was not a lot of time left. To be exact, I was given only weeks to prepare my family and all the other preparations that needed to be attended to before my deployment. Not only the things I point out here, but home services contracts and agreements had to be adjusted. I didn't feel that was enough time.

Then it was time to break the news to my employer. I had worked for the county for thirteen years, as a Detention officer. My captain could not believe the news and thought I was making it all up until I showed him the documents with departure dates and the length of time I would be deployed. That's when he and the others took the news more seriously, but still with some disbelief.

Within moments, the mood in the room changed and became somber. The captain, as well as my peers, let me know that I had their support and that they would do whatever they could to help make my transition from a civilian to full-time soldier smoother. Many said they would be praying for my family and me while I was away. There were some in the room who remained in disbelief. But, at least, my boss could move forward and find someone to replace me for the time I would be away.

Within days, I got a call from one of the personnel sergeants who was checking to ensure I had received instructions and departure dates. Before the sergeant stopped speaking, I had one last hope he would say he was aware I only had months left on my contract. Then it would have come down to, me not having enough time to serve in Iraq, and my military career would end according to my retirement plan. That would have meant I would not be deployed. However, it was not the case. Instead, he told me that the Army had adjusted my contract and extended my career another nine months. "Sergeant Slade, you will receive additional orders extending your contract in a couple of days."

My reserve contract was different from my regular army agreement, years earlier. My position in the army reserves was in comparison to working a part-time job, but more demanding. I was required to enlist for not less than three years, at least that was the minimum when I did my last enlistment. Another big difference, while serving in the reserves, I was obligated to attend monthly drills. Drills were required training sessions, which meant I trained one full weekend a month, and two-weeks once a year. I agreed to those basic requirements by signing my enlisted contract.

It was during the March drill when the Company Commander informed the rest of the soldiers that I was selected to deploy to Iraq in a few weeks. A military company is a military unit, with about 80 to 150 soldiers assigned to it. The Company Commander shared with everyone in the unit during the morning formation of the weekend drill, that he was as baffled as I was about my being selected for deployment. Once again, he emphasized the fact that he had no idea individual soldiers would be chosen.

The commander also informed me of additional information regarding my upcoming deployment. "Just want to let you know that there is an upcoming briefing in Charlotte, at Division Headquarters for you Sergeant Slade, and yes, the briefing is mandatory."

The Division is a much larger military unit, with as many as 10,000 to 20,000 soldiers assigned to it. Of course, the Division is broken down into units that are spread out among different regions. One week after being told by my local commander, I arrived in Charlotte for the briefing. Other soldiers from surrounding cities across the state showed up. I sat in a room feeling like a nervous father, waiting for the announcement of his firstborn. A tall Chaplin with thick white hair, wearing a sizeable cross on the outside of his uniform, entered into the briefing room. Following him was a cast of other individuals, some soldiers, and some civilians. They were there to counsel and process everyone who was being deployed through various stations.

I have to admit that a lot of useful information came out of the two-day event. I left Charlotte knowing a bit more of what to expect once I get to Iraq. Most of my time along with other soldiers who were present was spent standing in long lines, reviewing military personnel records. We had to ensure all documents were updated. Some of us received a brief physical to determine the status of our health. I received two shots on the second day, which left me with two very sore arms. The chief military nurse on duty pointed out that my blood pressure was a little high. It wasn't surprising to me, as anxious as I was.

The chief nurse also requested that I should bring an official document from my civilian doctor, reflecting the history of my blood pressure. He also stated, "depending on the results, there is a possibility of your deployment being put into question." Presenting that document could have had an impact on whether I would even be deployed. That was good news to me. It actually gave me some hope that I might not be deployed.

I returned the documents by mail, and just as fast as I mailed the documents, two days later I received a response. The medical doctor who examined my history, made a quick decision indicating that I was able to deploy. My blood pressure was borderline, but the doctor saw no problems at the time. Well, that was that, and marginal blood pressure would not be a factor in my deployment.

I was immediately granted leave from my job in order to prepare for deployment, which was important for my family and me. We were able to spend time together and talk about each other's concerns for the upcoming year. I spent my last days at home mentally preparing for my uncertain future. Then Thekla and I decided on a trip to Virginia Beach. The beach trip would give us a break, plus time to plan for deployment in a more relaxing environment.

We had been married for 25 years. My family members were nearby and offered their full support. However, my parents were well into their senior years and needed assistance themselves. My siblings were busy with their children and their careers. Thekla worked full time in a medical facility, where she had lots of support from her coworkers. The trip was good for us both. We were able to take time out to reflect on a few significant past events.

The following Monday, my journey into the unknown was to begin. I was up at 4:00 AM, and needed just an hour or two alone, before leaving home. I walked around the house, and out back to the garden. I wanted to say goodbye to my sanctuary, 'my space.' This was a place I would visit almost daily, for escapism, solitude, and meditation.

I had established a bird sanctuary back there a few years earlier. It included a flower garden and a vegetable garden, as well. Those were two places where I spent a lot of my free time. Because I was being deployed, it was going to be a while before I return to my garden. I prayed that it wouldn't be the last time I saw the place.

The sun had not risen, it was still dark, and I was trying to hold on to the night, not wanting the morning to come. Then I knew I would have to leave. But, morning eventually came. I tried to sneak back inside and not to disturb anyone. It didn't work, my family was up and gathered in the kitchen waiting for my return. We had our last breakfast together before the time came to leave.

The three of us loaded up into the car with all my luggage. Jamie followed in his truck, deciding that he would leave the airport to go directly to work. The drive to the airport was just over ten minutes from home, but that morning it seemed like hours. Another problem for me; was saying goodbye at airports. That has never been my thing.

This wasn't the first time I was deployed: we had gone through this twenty years ago when I received an assignment in South Korea. My children were much younger, and so was I. However, it did not make deploying any easier. Leaving my family behind to be deployed to any military operation has always been difficult. For the deployment to South Korea, Thekla made plans to take the kids with her to Germany, her home. Her friends and family members were nearby and were more than willing to help out. Besides, she felt much better being in Germany, where she could speak her own language and be among family and friends. She just thought that she would be more comfortable there, than alone in El Paso Texas.

Furthermore, knowing that she and the kids were in good hands, was reassuring to me. It was a totally different experience. The difference then was, I was not deploying to war. Leaving for war made everything much more difficult.

Everyone was teary-eyed, including me. The sky was gray and cloudy, the humidity was high from recent showers, and the whole environment was gloomy, matching my feelings. Jamie and Annika gathered my bags from the trunk of the car. Jamie told me he really wanted to be there with me. Thekla took the day off from work, and Annika chose to be a few hours late for school. As the minutes passed, my feelings grew heavier. Everyone fought back their tears. I wanted to run and jump right onto the plane to avoid the goodbyes, fearing I would break down. But I knew that would have been selfish and more hurtful for myself and my family.

We stood for a few moments saying our goodbyes. We managed to exchange a couple of smiles before the final hugs and kisses were given. I turned and began walking away towards the boarding gate. I was on my own. Walking towards the departing gate was almost too much. I walked through the security checkpoints and occasionally sneaking a peek back.

I completed the security checks and again looked through the glass wall. I saw both Thekla and Annika standing on the other side of the glass wall, wiping away tears. Glancing back one last time, I saw them slowly walking away.

Getting closer to the boarding gate, I notice three other soldiers who were waiting to board the plane. We were all associated with the same division, just different units. They too were on their way to Fort McCoy, with the final destination being Iraq. None of us were sure of the mission; we would have to wait until we arrive, to find that information out.

My seat was next to an Army captain. She introduced herself as a reservist from a unit out of Wilson NC. She told me that she was the mother of five children, which I found hard to believe because she looked so young. It was even harder to believe that she was being deployed, for reasons that she was a mother of five.

What was going on in the minds of those who made the decisions? How did they choose between who gets deployed, and who does not? A mother of five and an almost 50-year-old man were being sent off to a war-torn region. She would be gone for more than a year. Knowing how hard it was for me to leave my family, I felt heartbroken for her and her children.

After a period of conversing together, the two of us were able to pull ourselves together and calm down a bit. A short while into the flight, we found ourselves able to laugh a little. We shared information about our families and our civilian careers. It turned out that we had some things in common, and we had two mutual acquaintances. We exchanged email addresses, with the intention of keeping in touch while we were away. We continued the conversation going for a few hours, right up until the pilot announced that we should prepare for landing in Milwaukee, Wisconsin.

2

When we all walked off the plane, we were greeted by familiar faces: soldiers from our own Division Headquarters, who had left a day or two earlier. They were assigned to
meet us and assist with last-minute details. They had already set
up a mini processing station in the airport. More soldiers kept
showing up. Eventually, that whole wing of the terminal was
filled with soldiers who were all being deployed to Iraq. Each
one had their own unique look of bewilderment. No one knew
precisely what the next move was going to be.

We had to rush down to the lower level to retrieve our luggage, and return for a short briefing on the do's and don'ts.
We were briefed on travel plans and a timetable of events.
Also, we were given estimate times of departures and arrivals,
since we were traveling from the airport on chartered buses.
They named a few things that were off-limits, such as bars, no
purchasing alcohol, or leaving the wing of the terminal that we
were restricted to. They also expressed concern for everyone's
safety, since not everyone in the country was in support of the
war, and might target the military as retribution towards the
government.

After the briefing, we reported upstairs to the USO lounge
and waited for further instructions. It was the typical Army
thing: "hurry up and wait.".

While making our way up to the USO lounge, a small group
of girl scouts were lined up along the way. They handed each

soldier a box of Girl Scout cookies. This was their way of expressing their gratitude to us, for what we do for the country. Further along the way, there was another group lined up. They were senior citizens waving small U.S. flags, and thanking us for serving our great country. I put a smile on my face, but inside I was hurting. I wasn't in the celebratory mood. I had not yet gotten over leaving my family.

This was a significant moment in my life. I was on my way to war, and I just couldn't shake my somber mood. My way of life was now different. I was among all these strangers who were coming up to me and expressing their gratitude, and thanking me for serving the country. We received lots of recognition, and appreciation from all kinds of folks that day. It was a little overwhelming. Even from those civilians who did not express their gratitude, I could somehow feel that they too were giving us a nod of approval. I still had no idea at the time of exactly how I would be serving the country.

I knew it wasn't the right place or time, but in my mind, I questioned the whole ordeal. Neither did I know the exact reason why the country was at war. I just didn't buy the weapons of mass destruction argument. I believed that there were other reasons for the war. I did have a lot of questions about the war. One being who benefited the most from my services to the country? Was it the CEOs of the oil companies, or the citizens like those who stood in the airport? The country was divided on the validity of this war, and so was my mind.

From both, my life and military experience, I didn't understand. Also, from my point of view, the intelligence briefings and the reasons given to the public for invading Iraq were not genuine. Neither was I willing to accept what we were being told. My gut feeling told me it was about the oil.

It was next to impossible for me not to second guess the war and my deployment. I wondered if the other soldiers who I was surrounded by, took time out to think over the real rationale of why we were going to Iraq. There were several different explanations given by the leaders of the government. The government argued that Sadam Hussein, the president of Iraq, had chemical weapons. Then there were the congressional and military leaders who told the world, that we were going in to liberate a group of oppressed people and free them from dictatorship. The opposition argued that President G.W. Bush's storming of Iraq in March 2003, was his way of getting revenge for his father. The senior President G.H. Bush went to war with Iraq in January 1991, without any success of his own. I guessed it was a thing of who you believed.

Soldiers were deployed from every state in the union, and from all walks of life. A majority of the soldiers were far more excited and willing to go to Iraq than I was. Some soldiers were even prepared to give their lives for their country without giving it a second thought. They proudly executed the orders given. Some were more excited over extra pay than they were for their safety.

The impression I got from many of the soldiers who were deployed along with me, was that they firmly believed they were doing a good cause for their God and their country. I honor both their principles and attitudes. They responded without questions. I honestly believe that in their hearts they felt that they were doing the right thing. They wanted to be respectful to both their government and to their leadership. I was the outsider who was trying to fit in with the majority. I am not indicating that I didn't respect my government or my leaders, what I am suggesting is that I had a different point of view. I too had sworn to obey and execute the orders given to me by my superiors.

It had been a few years since I was surrounded by so many highly motivated soldiers on active duty and wearing the uniform. When I arrived at the USO lounge, again I was hailed by another group of patriotic citizens, showing how proud they were of all soldiers in the unit. They were an older generation of patriots as well. Given the geographical location of the airport,

13

most of the participants were white males. I later discovered that they were retired army officers and NCOs. NCO is the acronym for Non-Commissioned officers, higher rank of enlisted members. The military uses volumes of abbreviations.

The retired soldiers were volunteers along with their spouses. They seemed thrilled to serve us and vowed to do whatever they could to make us comfortable. After interacting with the volunteers for a short period, I believed, that they believed more in the mission than I did. They were indeed more excited than I was. They went all out to collect books, cell phones, and computers for us to enjoy, or to contact our families. With smiles on their faces, they prepared hotdogs, sandwiches, drinks, and other refreshments for everyone.

Since 9/11 I have heard more about this generation of Americans, but it was a group that I had never had any experiences with. I learned right away that you don't have to wear a uniform to serve your country. These Americans were different from those back in the Southeast. At least that was my first impression. They displayed their patriotism proudly. They let it be known how proud they were of us and thanked us for everything. I certainly thanked them for their hospitality.

Nearly four hours had passed before a sergeant came up to the USO lounge, and announced that we were departing.

"Listen up everyone, it's time to depart the terminal. I need all soldiers to grab your bags and load up on one of the chartered buses that are lined up outside."

More loyal senior citizens stood in the terminal, waving flags and saying their goodbyes. They continued to assure us that the citizens of America were behind us. I had come to admire that group of Americans. Nearly all soldiers, including myself, waved back, smiling to thank them for their support and kind gestures. Some of my most difficult steps of the journey were behind me, I was moving on.

We loaded onto the buses and continued on our journey to Fort McCoy. I went back to thinking about how my family must have been feeling. There wasn't anything that I could do but pray that they would be okay. As I prayed, I also prayed for those who sat on the bus with me. Every seat on the bus was filled, and three more buses were trailing us, completely full. Listening to the many diverse conversations and watching the soldiers on the bus, I discovered that some pretty interesting folks were being deployed. The majority of soldiers on the bus were also professional citizens from all walks of life. There was a banker, a medical doctor, a superintendent of schools, and several police officers. The majority were from the southeastern states.

The journey reminded me of earlier years in the army. Back then I was taking a bus from Columbia, South Carolina, down to Augusta, Georgia, to begin eight weeks of advanced training. Some years later I was on a bus trip to Fort McCoy to start another eight weeks of military training.

I felt pretty anxious as the buses rolled closer to the fort, while many other soldiers remained heavily engaged in their conversations. I assumed that it was their way of diverting their minds from reality. Many soldiers knew each other from working together at previous locations and meeting elsewhere, throughout their military career.

Still, there were a few of us on the bus who were complete strangers. Yet, in reality, there were no strangers, because we were all united by the uniform that we wore. That's something that was instilled in our minds early in our careers, "we are a team." Regardless of race, sex, creed, or background, we were all equal, according to the rules of conduct. We were representatives of an "Army of one."

Curiosity then replaced the conversations that everyone was having. Nearly everyone got quiet and began to check out the scenes outside the extra-large dark tinted windows on the bus. The bus slowed and inched closer to the gates of Fort Mc-Coy. I saw many old white wooden buildings, identical to each other, two stories, with red and black tile roofs. Each building sat on gray brick block piers. Several of the buildings seemed to be in the process of renovation to make room for more troops, the driver told those of us who were seated up front, "many more soldiers will be coming for training."

The bus came to a halt, and a tall sergeant wearing a desert battle dress (BDU) 'chocolate chip uniform' stepped on the bus. "Welcome to Fort McCoy." He used his rich baritone voice, to capture everyone's attention. "This will be your home for the next sixty or more days." Then he turned to the driver, giving him directions to one of the buildings, before continuing to welcome us.

With the other buses following, the bus started moving slowly for almost a quarter of a mile before pulling into the parking lot of a one-story red brick building and stopping. It was a one-level building with red brick and large tinted windows around the entrance. It was a relatively new building in comparison to the other buildings we passed only a few blocks back.

"Everyone should get off, and unload your luggage!" The sergeant shouted. There was a smile on the face of the sergeant, which was an indication to me that he enjoyed his job.

Eight more soldiers stood on the ground wearing desert camouflage uniforms (DCUs) were waiting to greet us. They were known as the advance party, meaning they deployed a few weeks earlier than the group of soldiers I traveled with. Their mission was to arrive early and prepare the logistics for our stay at the fort. The advance party soldiers would become our guides for the next sixty days of training. As soon as our feet hit the ground, they too began shouting out instructions.

"Gather your luggage and place it in one section of the parking lot in four neat rows. You will be able to gather it after the briefing. Now everyone should quickly move inside." We moved inside the building and took a seat at one of the tables. The tables were in rows, jammed tightly together. To say it was a tight fit, would be an understatement. Every one of us from all four buses were crammed into that small room. As soon as we were seated, I wanted it to be over. It was most uncomfortable sitting so close together and reviewing documents.

I couldn't believe that there was a need for more information. Just as we finished the paperwork, we were assigned to teams and sleeping quarters. The team that you were attached to also represented the personnel that you lived with and trained with while at Fort McCoy. One of your team members became your "battle buddy." A battle buddy was someone that you trusted and leaned on for almost everything throughout your stay at Fort McCoy. Every soldier was advised to pick a buddy and get to know him or her.

I was a little reluctant to get too close to anyone so fast, for fear of selecting someone totally different than I was. But there was no one like me present. I was looking for someone that I could just talk with, not really someone to share secrets with. Your battle buddy would know all or most of all about you. They were supposed to know where you were at all times, and even a few personal things. The army wanted the battle buddy to be a close relationship between two soldiers. That someone should get to know you well. They even wanted the battle buddy to know things like your date of birth, marriage date, where you were born, how many kids, etc. To me, this was sharing (TMI) too much information.

Having a battle buddy was not a bad idea. By pairing up with a battle buddy, the army was trying to prevent soldiers from feeling alone, depressed, and more important to prevent suicide. The welfare of the soldier was important. The military wanted the soldier to know that there was someone there, if there was ever a need. From that perspective, having a battle buddy was a good thing. But, I was somewhat of an introvert, and it was difficult allowing someone to enter too closely into my space.

At midlife, neither was I excited about some stranger getting into my personal affairs. For those reasons, I left the briefing room without choosing a battle buddy.

We all left the briefing room and gathered our luggage, walking a few yards over to what was to be our living quarters. We took the shortcut, by jumping a ditch beside the roadway. Jumping the ditch with everything I brought with me on my back, was a little difficult. But I made it, and we reached the outdated World War II barracks and rushed in through both the front and back doors. Everyone on the team moved quickly to claim a small dull gray, metal frame twin bunk with an old worn mattress. I was able to land the second bunk on the left, near the door. I felt lucky about being near the door and the wall.

There was no bother at all by not having a neighbor on my right side. To be exact, it worked out well, giving me a little more privacy. Some soldiers chose to live upstairs on the second floor. The floor between us was so hollow that I was able to hear nearly every spoken word and every step that was taken up there. The same can be said for spaces separating the wooden boards on the walls. I could see the light shining in from the outside. The cool breeze was no exception, it blew right through the open cracks.

I found no reason to complain about the living conditions. I was excited about having a place to crash after so many hours of traveling, and the time spent being briefed. For sixty days those old wooden barracks would become my home, and I was determined to make the best of it. It had been well beyond ten years since I had slept in the barracks. I had grown comfortable sleeping in my king-size bed back home. This was another challenge that I had to overcome. At my age, it wasn't easy readjusting my lifestyle and having to live under rules and guidelines.

About the battle buddy situation, I still didn't commit, even after being pushed by my sergeant. I let him know that I was close to choosing someone that I had in mind. I needed to check with my potential battle buddy first, and then I would inform my sergeant as soon as I did. For me, it was noteworthy that the average age of the soldiers assigned to our team was about thirty-five. That was saying a lot about how the army had changed in terms of age and the type of soldiers who were selected to go to Iraq. The youngest guy was twenty-three, and the oldest was fifty-nine. There were guys on the team who were my age and older, but I still was not quite ready to choose a battle buddy, so I just kind of went with the flow of things for as long as I could.

For three long days, we spent hours standing in line having our personal and medical records thoroughly examined. Attention needed to be given to a specific protocol ensuring that all documents were correct, and everyone's health met the requirements for deployment. There was still a chance that the army would find something wrong with my health that would prevent me from being deployed. At the medical facility at Fort McCoy, I thought for sure if the officials determined something was wrong with me, they would send me home. Like before, my physical checked out okay, and I was cleared for deployment. It's likely that it was meant to be.

3

It was intolerable; we spent an entire afternoon stuffed in a small room while we were given information and assigned to training teams. At one point it even became difficult to breathe. I was squeezed in between two guys who weighed well over 200 pounds each. Once we were dismissed from the room, it took a few moments before I was able to breathe normally.

The group went inside as one large unorganized cluster of soldiers. When we were dismissed, we emerged as three large organized teams. There were close to thirty soldiers assigned to each team. The teams were identified by the colors; red, white, and blue. The team members were selected according to their job titles, and the mission they were chosen for.

I was assigned to the red team. I had a positive first impression of the majority of soldiers that were on the team. My team members were the same individuals that I would live and train with throughout my stay at Fort McCoy. The teams were well diverse; however, there were still a few small groups of "buddies," who stuck to themselves for various reasons.

I spent my first evening with other members of my team in the barracks, unpacking and trying to get acquainted with each other. I ended up listening to a couple of guys jabber away over the housing conditions and not having enough storage space. I had plenty, the storage of personal property was a small issue. The two guys were not pleased that the only place to secure their personal belongings, was by storing it in a single footlocker at the bottom of the bunk.

The more significant issue was that in a few weeks we would be deployed to a warzone. I didn't consider the two soldiers' complaint about the lack of storage space even legitimate. Who knows what they thought when they packed? They packed as if they were moving into a college dorm, not like they were packing for a military training camp. It was their own fault that they didn't have enough space.

I crammed the few books, laptop and smaller items I brought along into the footlocker as best as I could. We were restricted from wearing civilian clothes until after we returned from Iraq. Therefore, I left my civilian clothes packed away in my suitcase underneath my bunk. No soldier wants to go on a journey without packing at least one change of civilian clothes. Some commanders will order soldiers to fly in civilian clothing as a matter of safety. Then too, there was always the possibility that we might have gotten a pass to go into town. That never happened, since most of our time was dedicated to training.

The guys who were doing all the complaining were just unhappy about being there. They complained about everything. They started on living conditions and ended up complaining about the weather. I wondered if they were thinking that their room was going to be in a five-star hotel. And Lord knows, no one had any control of the weather.

It was June, but the weather felt like February. During the briefing, members of the staff hinted that Wisconsin was much colder than what we were accustomed to in the southeast. The nights were cool and the mornings were quite nippy. As long as the showers were warm I had no problem, I could adjust to the weather.

I was determined to succeed; I began adjusting to my new life one step at a time. The first weeks were quite challenging. The images of my family standing in the airport continued to resurface. In the meantime, I was stuck living with thirty plus

21

men, all who were far different than I was. I knew from the first day forward that it wasn't going to be comfortable living in an open bay. It had been years since I slept with a group of soldiers under those conditions. Now after more than ten years, I was doing it all over again.

One of the first rules that we voted on as a group was when the lights are to be turned off. I voted with the minority. We wanted the lights off at 2100 hours, 9:00 p.m. The group of soldiers I voted with lost the vote. The lights would remain on until 2200 hours, that would be 10:00 p.m. The lights going off at 10:00 p.m. didn't prevent some of the soldiers from pacing up and down the floor. They could easily see how to find their way from the street light that was beaming through the windows.

Following the period of getting everyone settled down, the administrative staff laid out the agenda for the next few weeks. The very next day we went right into training, where things began to intensify. The training personnel never let us forget why we were there, as they began laying out the overall mission. The start of each day was at 0500 hours. Beginning with physical fitness training, breakfast, and clean-up of the barracks. Then it was off to the business of the day, whether it was in the classroom, or in the field.

Each morning, there was an accountability formation, and at the same time, a health and welfare check was conducted. At the end of the day, the formation was less formal. We had team huddles to inform and update everyone on all upcoming events. Sometimes it seemed as if the commander would never stop talking. His Q&A sessions were long and drawn out. But one thing was for sure, we were always on top of any news referencing training or deployment.

Then there were the nurses who would not stop interfering with my training. They continued to monitor my blood pressure. According to them, my blood pressure was fluctuating, and they thought it could have been an issue that might have prevented me from being deployed. I got pretty weary listening to all the information that the nurses kept telling me. Who knowns, maybe their very presence contributed to the rise of my blood pressure. When they were not present my blood pressure, as well as my attitude, was okay. I was at a point, where I was hoping that everything would check out okay and I would be cleared for deployment.

It was time to get with the program or I would have a lot of catching up to do. Waiting around for the nurses to make their recommendation on my deployment was an emotional rollercoaster. Finally, I came to my own resolution. I was not going to allow my medical issues to continue to be a distraction. I psyched myself up for the mission to do my best to prepare for the endeavor. I repeatedly told myself that I would be deploying. There was a possibility that things could have changed, but I wasn't about to wait around for the news. I needed to be prepared for whatever the outcome. That meant working harder to get into proper mental and physical condition.

Each hour spent standing in line presented an opportunity to build onto relationships that I already started with my "barracks buddies." Because we came from all walks of life, we talked about a wide variety of topics which was always interesting. We talked mostly about family issues and of course, being deployed. Although we were a large group of individuals, I did not hear anyone bring up politics. Neither did I hear anyone speak a negative word, about the country being at war.

In all likelihood, it was due to the overall training that soldiers received early on. There are army regulations in place that advise against soldiers being too opinionated, about army policies, or their chain of command. Depending on how a soldier addresses some issues regarding the military, it's possible they could find themselves facing severe judicial problems. If one does happen to receive some sort of retribution for speaking out, then it is also possible for the soldier to be discharged from the military. For those reasons alone, no soldier wanted to cross that line.

I am not saying that there weren't soldiers with concerns or opinions, they just didn't voice them publicly. Soldiers hardly ever spoke out or expressed their personal views over decisions that were made by (DA) Department of the Army. At least that was the way it was back in the early years of my training. However, there was a small percentage of individuals who did speak out against the war, and even the leadership, but only as a tactic of trying to prevent deployment. Those soldiers were seeking a discharge, regardless of the severity of the outcome.

I worked hard to adjust to regular army life again. As difficult as it was, quite frequently I bit my tongue to hold back my opinion. I saw first-hand, the problems of being too opinionated could have caused. For those reasons, I chose not to squabble over politics. Especially during a time of deployment.

On the last day of long lines, I was notified that I had to return back to the medical station, only this time it was routine. Everyone had to be examined by a medical doctor one final time. The final examination was supposed to be the one that counted. While the exam was being conducted, I was a little tense, to put it mildly. Regardless, I no longer had mixed feelings over the deployment. When it was time for me to have my blood pressure checked, the reading was high, which was no surprise to me. Only a week had passed already, since being prescribed medication to get my blood pressure under control.

The doctor wanted to monitor my blood pressure for an additional five days. A decision then would be made at a later date to determine if I still qualified medically for the deployment. I had already made up my mind that I was deploying no matter what. I was not going to allow the medical staff to muddle up my mind. Again, they were putting me back on observation. Their method was confusing. Nevertheless, without further questions, I just complied with their course of action.

I began to alter my attitude and moved forward in terms of deployment. I focused more on the training and becoming proficient in being a full-time soldier. Getting back to the routine of exercising, slightly improved my blood pressure after a few days. The only time I saw the medical staff again was for routine checks, along with the other soldiers on the team. After that, I began to focus more on the long days and intensive hours of training ahead.

Next up was classrooms instructions, which consisted mostly of power points and film. These were dubbed "death by PowerPoint," by a group of soldiers. That was their way of letting the instructor know that information was starting to become dull and repetitious. Many soldiers in the room started falling asleep, including me. A number of us placed wagers on who would be the first to fall asleep. Staying awake became a struggle. Sleep was sacred. Returning to class in the evenings and not being released until 2200 hours was not easy.

I was thankful we didn't have to march to class. In addition to all other training in a soldier's day, marching from one location to another was common. There were sites that we could have walked to, but since we were operating on a tight schedule, time was of the essence. One favorable advantage we had were buses which carried us almost anywhere we needed to go on the post.

On standby were a few buses whose primary mission was to transport us to and from training sites. There were training locations in all corners of Ft McCoy. Distance from the main post headquarters, where Forward Operating Bases (FOB). They were designed to provide the most realistic training of Iraq possible. A majority of the training was conducted at the FOBs, including a few overnight classes.

In comparison to all other training, I think the most essential instruction given, was the introduction to the infamous "Improvised Explosive Devices," (IEDs). These devices were designed to be triggered by many different items, such as cell phones, and gadgets hidden inside coke cans, dead animals, empty rocket shells, old tires, and anything else that could be used to conceal the explosives.

IED training underscored one of the deadliest devices used by militants against the coalition forces. IEDs alone were responsible for a majority of the deaths involving US personnel in Iraq and Afghanistan. With a minimal amount of training, we were expected to become as proficient as possible on how to identify these weapons. The enemy's favorite targets were tactical vehicles driven by American personnel. Civilian vehicles that were making deliveries to any of the NATO camps were no exception. We were told that research was continually being conducted to find ways to prevent, or at least decrease, the amount of damage that IED attacks caused.

A selected number of the training films were exaggerated with highlights to emphasize the impact that the IEDs had on soldiers and the government as a whole. The film footage was orchestrated with hits of rock music played loudly in the background to dramatize the already horrible images of people being blown up. It was a little difficult to digest some of what I saw on the screen. I knew the music was meant to influence the thinking of soldiers. It was the instructor's way of captivating the younger soldiers.

Nearly all of the instructors themselves were young, and they thought the idea of using music was cool. It was a psychological strategy that they choose to use to influence the class. After watching the film, I was deeply concerned, but the music technique had no influence on my thinking. The message that the video conveyed was harsh, but it was the reality.

It didn't take a lot to convince me about how important the information was to my survival. I was one of many who tried to grasp as much information as possible. Especially when it came to responding to the explosions. It was only a matter of weeks before I would likely be an occupant in a military vehicle convoying through Iraq. Learning survival tips from those who had experienced these deadly attacks was the best training that the army could offer at the time. I took advantage of every life-saving tip that was given. I worried that a couple of days of training was not enough time to learn about them.

Times had indeed changed, the training was way more advanced than the training I received at the beginning of my career. It was more technical and done at a faster pace. I put my trust in all that I was taught, and those who were teaching it. They were the experts, and they had the experience with what they were teaching. I was grateful that they shared their expertise with us. But, I prayed that I would never have to experience the things that they had.

I am sure that the army did its research before bringing soldiers like myself back onto active duty. I always thought the army wanted to invest in a much younger and leaner soldier. I assumed that it no longer mattered. It was apparent that the recruiting process had slowed. It had gotten to a point where reserve soldiers were selected on a 'desperate for demand basis.' It was surprising to discover that the army could still use guys my age in combat. I was amazed that they believed we old cronies could perform the tactical tasks that were required of soldiers in warfare.

Reservists have always been required to stay fit, and maintain their knowledge of military skills, just as active-duty soldiers are required to do. The primary purpose of the monthly drills and the two weeks of annual training is to keep guys like me up to par. The army wants its reserve soldiers to be as combat ready as its active-duty soldiers. Nevertheless, after reviewing some of the training films, I felt nothing could prepare me for the action that I may encounter in Iraq. Many years had passed since I last participated in any type of intensive training. The first few weeks of training at Fort McCoy certainly let me know that there were some tasks that I needed to be retrained in.

I noticed the difference between everyday soldiers, and the weekend warriors right away. Although both groups trained hard, there are different mindsets between the two groups. Older soldiers like me have more experience, but the older we get, the more we begin to lose focus. Especially, after reaching the last year of our career. We started looking forward to the future, as we prepare for life after the army.

Looking around at the soldiers that I was in training with, more than half didn't seem to be in the best physical condition. Nevertheless, they were there, and more than willing to do their part. A surprising number of the trainers at Fort McCoy were National Guard and Reservists as well. Many of them had never deployed into a combat zone. However, they were skillful enough to qualify to teach the specifics that we needed to know, to fight a war. They taught from the field manual, not from experience. Some soldiers questioned the non-combat trainer's abilities. Likewise, I preferred the guys who had combat experience.

The instructors with the most experience were on their third and fourth tour of duty in Iraq and Afghanistan. It was an unusual time to be in the army. Lots of training had to be revised almost daily to keep up with the tactics that were being used by the enemy. In some ways, the trainers were the messengers. They did the best that they could with the information that was given to them. Like all of the soldiers who played a role in the deployment, they had to remain flexible. Those few Iraq war veterans who were chosen to be instructors, stood out. I paid full attention to those men and women. They were convincing and shared useful advice on how to survive, based on their own experiences.

Like any other army base, Fort McCoy was more than just a training camp. Additional military operations were carried out there. I ran into a couple of recruiters at Fort McCoy who were there to recruit soldiers for special duties in Iraq. They shared the difficulties of recruiting soldiers to reenlist or extend their tours in the army. I assume that's how I ended up at Fort McCoy myself. There was likely a shortage of personnel to fill the ranks.

The hours of combat training were long. That's not including the time I spent in the cultural and language classes. 'Not me,' was my initial reaction to the language class. I thought it was a bit too late for me to learn another language. It was a struggle trying to keep up with the younger generation of soldiers in the room. I just couldn't get it. The handouts that we were given on those two subjects didn't help a lot either. I did my best and studied the handouts thoroughly whenever time permitted. It was mentally exhausting trying to retain so much information in such a short time.

The army felt that it was important for soldiers to learn about the Iraqi culture. The culture training class was supposed to introduce us to how everyday Iraqis live. The course also touched on how we as soldiers should conduct ourselves while in Iraq.

I wanted to be a team player, and I worked hard to be successful in becoming one. I tried to fit. More importantly, I wanted to survive. I believed the only way to survive was to become as skillful as I possibly could in everything that was being taught. When it came to learning the language, it was even more challenging. All I could do was try.

During one training session that took place in the barracks, Colonel Sam said we were getting two new additions to the team. No fault of their own, but they were showing up a few weeks later. It was a surprise to learn that one of the guys was Clayton, a member of my reserve unit back in North Carolina. Clayton was coming to join the red team. I was probably one of the few soldiers deployed to have a coworker and neighbor deployed with me. More noteworthy it was kind of nice knowing someone that I knew would be taking the same journey.

Sometime before I left the unit, I recall Clayton telling me that he would be coming up to Fort McCoy. Despite his saying he would be joining us, I never expected to run into him because of the size of the place. I don't think he expected to run into me either. I greeted Clayton at the door of the barracks and gave him a hand with his luggage. I assisted him in finding a place to settle down. I escorted him up the stairs to one of the last two empty bunks. Unlike me, Clayton was excited about joining the team.

For some of the reasons mentioned, Clayton and I were acquaintances, but not to close. He was twenty-three years younger than I was. However, what I knew of him over the years, Clayton was an excellent and very likable guy. He was married and had four small children. I later found out that he volunteered for duty in Iraq, which explained his excitement about coming on board.

Clayton and I were from totally different backgrounds and had different views on the war in general. I very much respected his opinions, and he showed much respect for mine. We certainly had different goals in mind in terms of our military careers, as well. My mind was made up that as soon as I return from Iraq, my military career would be over. Clayton's future goals were much different than mine. He wanted to remain in the army at least another four years, if not longer.

Clayton loved the military and being an infantry soldier. Our deployment status also affected us differently. I don't believe it bothered him as much as it did me. At least he didn't give that impression. Despite the two of us starting out on our deployment together, we eventually were split up, because of our military occupation skills. He was a combat infantryman, and I was a communications specialist, as well as a logistics specialist.

I soon discovered that Clayton was not the only soldier who volunteered for duty in Iraq. There were other soldiers that I met, who also volunteered to go to Iraq. Nevertheless, I was even more surprised at the number of guys who volunteered for financial reasons. They were in it for the extra combat pay, that would be added to their monthly salaries. The more I got to know the other soldiers, the more amazed I was at some of the stories they shared about their military career.

Many of the soldiers at Fort McCoy were there preparing for deployment. Most of them had already gone beyond the twenty years that were required for retirement. There were a few that could have walked away from the military before being deployed. They were the ones who were there for reasons other than financial reasons. They felt that it was their patriotic duty to be deployed. For them, going to war was the right thing to do for their God and their country.

I certainly didn't feel that motivated at the time. I was there because of my contract, and the agreement that I swore to uphold. Although, I never thought I would be training for war just as I started planning for my retirement.

4

The closer we got to completing the training, the more anxious I became. "Soldiers, I want to let you know that the division commander and a few other staff members have been collaborating with our sister unit in Iraq. Those are the soldiers that we're going to relieve in a few weeks," Colonel Sam, the Platoon Leader, informed us.

The division commander sent a message to the unit commander in Iraq informing him that soon we will be on our way to replace his soldiers. And of course, they were happy to receive the news. "They can hardly wait for our arrival," Colonel Sam also told us. He emphasized the importance of everyone being qualified in all areas before he could report that all training had been completed. "Let's go do this," he said.

Each platoon commander agreed that it was better to complete all training a few days early rather than rush in the end. He wanted everyone to have a few free days before we were to deploy. No one argued with him on that subject.

Our days at Fort McCoy were limited. Colonel Sam's remarks "Let's go do this," stuck with me for the rest of that day. Since our first meeting I began to notice a change in his voice, more so after weeks of robust training. He gave a short speech to the platoon, and his voice sounded like war drums. He spoke as if he was trying to pump us up for battle. Perhaps the colonel was reacting to his feelings about being deployed to Iraq, after recently returning from Afghanistan.

After Colonel Sam's briefing, we all agreed to hustle and finish up the training. "Yeah, let's do this," I said to a comrade. I was pushing myself and psyching myself up, trying hard to prepare mentally for the mission in Iraq.

We rushed to get to the arms room to pick up our weapons. The arms room was the most secure room on the fort. It was required that all firearms and ammunition be stored inside the heavily secured room, and could only be accessed by authorized personnel. Once everyone signed for their weapons, we were on our way to the M4 rifle range. It was mandatory that everyone qualified with both the M4 and the M9 handgun. Once that happened, we were a step closer to the completion of all training. The team stood as one. That being the case, everyone gladly helped their battle buddy finish up. I teamed up with Sergeant Todd, who eventually became my battle buddy.

I was a little nervous about qualifying. I didn't consider myself a good shooter. It was more important to me that I was able to hit the live targets. I never liked the idea of having to prove myself by shooting targets for a score. It reminded me of standardized testing. What did it prove? Everyone tests differently, and so it was with the shooting.

Before linking back up with the Army Reserve, I had a ten-year break from the military. I probably could have used the break as an excuse for my poor shooting skills. I could also associate my lack of skills to age, and changes to my eyesight as well. At the time, I thought those were fairly good excuses for my poor shooting. I wasn't worried about not qualifying and being left behind. If I had not completed all training, it would have resulted in being left back. It would have also ended my journey, or maybe my military career. My mind was made up, I was going to give my best in trying to qualify with both weapons. If by chance I would not have qualified, and not been deployed, then I would have been seen as a loser by some.

However, what helped me was the laser that was attached to my M4 rifle. That tool did what it was designed to do. It was supposed to increase the accuracy of the weapon, and boy did it! I am proof that it works; I hit my targets. It was the very first time in my twenty-year career that I shot as well as I did. After zeroing in on the targets with the new laser guide, I hit a record number of 30 out of 32 targets. Some did better, but I was pleased. That relieved me of the tension that I created for myself before coming to the firing range. At least now, I was able to do something right. I qualified at the shooting range as an expert.

I have to give a lot of credit for my shooting so well to the civilian trainer. He was right by my side coaching me along. He did an excellent job of motivating me while I was shooting. He told me: "Relax, breathe and take your time. You can do it," and I did.

On the ride back from the range I sat with Major M. He was somewhere around his mid-thirties. He too was an army reservist and worked as a police officer in Atlanta Georgia. In the army, he was a logistics officer. He was on the bus with me when we departed the airport in Milwaukee. Often there were times when we would get together and talk about the deployment, and about life as a law enforcement officer.

Major M. was a nice guy, and I enjoyed talking with him when time permitted. He had recently completed his studies at the war college. Unlike my own selection for deployment, he was chosen for other reasons. Because he was fresh out of the war college, he wasn't surprised that he was selected for deployment.

Another respectable career soldier who I had the honor of meeting as soon as we returned from the range, was Master Sergeant W. (MSG) He worked on the training team at Fort McCoy. He was an active duty sergeant, who was assigned from Ft Bragg. I found him to be quite a professional soldier and more importantly, a very opinionated individual. Not everyone would agree. Some of his peers, sergeant majors and first sergeants, as well as some of the officers on the team, did not agree with his opinion at times. However, he performed his duties proficiently.

Master Sergeant W. admitted that his job was frustrating at times, because some guys went out of their way to make things difficult for him. He shared a story with me about a particular experience he had while in Iraq two years earlier. He'd befriended a young soldier, who was very troubled and had joined the army to change his life. However, the young soldier had problems with some of the members in his company as well. The master sergeant talked about how that one incident will probably remain with him for the rest of his life. "The young soldier was determined to get things right. He wanted to make his leaders proud of him." At the same time, he was making those decisions, the fighting in Iraq grew more intense, and the patrols increased. The young soldier came to him and said, "I don't think that I can make it."

"Sure, you can. Just pray and ask your God to help you," the Master Sergeant W. told the younger soldier.

The young soldier responded to Master Sergeant W. and said: "I saw myself in the future, and heard a distant voice saying that everything is going to be alright."

It was just before the young soldier went out on his next mission. Later that same night when it was time for his team to return, he never did. He was killed in action during a gunfight in Baghdad.

Master Sergeant W. told me the incident changed both his views on war and life. "War is a very dire operation, and we must never forget to pray and evaluate ourselves from time to time. Especially when we find ourselves in difficult situations."

After listening to the story from the master sergeant, my heart sank. I asked myself why did he tell me the story? The master sergeant said it was his way of saying, "Stay strong, stay focused, and most importantly: always stay prayed up, and come back home. There will be low points and challenges, but

keep your head up and your eyes on the prize, which is returning home safe. You will get through it."

I thanked him for his advice, but truthfully, I was more
worried about my future after listening to his about the young
soldier. However, I decided that I was not going to worry about
things I had no control over. I was preparing to face whatever
it was that I had to face. "All I could do was, all I could do."
Primarily I had to continue to have confidence in both my God
and the trainers.

Unexpectedly, we were ahead of schedule. This allowed
us to have more downtime, which was certainly needed and
appreciated. We had the opportunity to take care of some personal matters. There was laundry to be caught up on, shopping
at the Post Exchange (PX) for a few hygiene items, or just to get
a break away from the barracks.

I used the time wisely by not laying around worrying about
the future. I spent much of my free time alone, exploring my
surroundings and wandered off into different places on the
fort. For about an hour a day, I hung out in one of the computer
labs, hoping to catch up on emails and the news from around
the world. Everyone else seemed to be doing their own thing as
well. Some watched DVDs, others spent time in the gym, at the
movies, and a few of the guys slept their time away.

It was the twenty-third day of May already, and my son's
twenty-fourth birthday. I remember the time when I wanted
him to follow my footsteps and join the military. Looking back,
I am relieved that he didn't take my advice. I was glad that it
was me who was being deployed, and not him. My son was
more focused and determined then I was when I was his age.
He had other ideas and chose to travel a different road in his
life. It was never on his mind to consider to join the military.

The eight weeks of retraining certainly took a toll on me,
both mentally and physically. My body seemed to agree with
my idea of ending my military career soon. I was constantly
recovering from some physical tasks that I was required to

perform. The pain let me know that my body was not up to spending another year of my life in the military. This time I was more serious, after the deployment, I was truly wrapping it up.

I had other ambitions that I wanted to experience. There was no way I wanted to continue on with my military career. I had reached milestone after milestone, and it was time to prepare for closure.

The platoon leaders hinted that if everyone completed training in enough time, it was possible we could get a short pass to go home. Hearing that news was bigger than any motivational speech or pep rally up until that point. Not only did the division commander want everyone trained for war, but he also wanted everyone to have a break from training, and get a few days of rest.

We started to enjoy the final days at Fort McCoy. We had moved into a period of waiting. I was happy the training was coming to an end. There were days when I only had a few hours of training. The training was nothing like when we started out. It lasted two hours at the most. That allowed for more time for myself. Many of the soldiers in the platoon had already completed all of their training.

From my trips to the Morale, Welfare, and Recreation Center, and watching TV, as well as browsing the internet, I realized that the news from Iraq was not good. Waves of sectarian violence had spread across the country. As a result, numerous soldiers and Iraqi civilians were killed almost daily.

Before sunset, I would walk around the post, trying to walk off a few calories and relax my mind, after the last meal of the day. Walking was an excellent way for me to calm all the anxieties that I had built up since the weeks I left home. Learning new people, places, and skills had all happened in a matter of weeks. Not to mention that I was expected to learn a different language.

Jokingly, I used my southern accent as an excuse not to learn to speak Arabic, citing that I spoke with a very slow tongue. That being the case, there was no way I would be able to pronounce the Arabic terms correctly. Honestly, I had no desire to learn it. In hindsight, it was probably another way of protesting against my deployment.

However, later I realized that learning the language could be a significant tool for survival. Learning about the Arabic culture was also intended to help with relationship building. At least the Iraqis would see that I was trying to communicate. In the end, I changed my attitude and became more open to learning Arabic.

I stopped by the PX for a cup of tea and found a seat on a nearby bench to soak up some Wisconsin sunshine. While sitting there, a young female sergeant approached me and asked if the spot next to me was free. She was tall and attractive with a dark complexion, and neatly dressed in her combat uniform. She introduced herself as Sergeant Law and said she had just returned from a one-year tour in Iraq. This was her first day back in the States. Wow! And with a look of amazement all over my face, was my reaction to what she just told me. I let her know that I would be leaving for Iraq within a few days.

"Not meaning to be an annoyance, but I really would like to ask you a few questions about your tour in Iraq," I said to her.

"I have no problem with you asking me questions," she pleasantly replied.

I am not sure if Sergeant Law understood. I wanted to know everything. I wanted to know about her emotions, and how she survived her year-long tour. The sergeant was very kind and willing to talk about her experience. I suppose even more at that point since it was all behind her. She explained that she was a medic who worked and lived in the now-infamous Abu Ghraib prison camp. It was reported that some American soldiers had abused Iraqi prisoners there.

I found Sergeant Law to be a highly intellectual individual. She later disclosed that she was a full-time high school teacher in Jamaica and part-time army reservist. She disagreed with the reasons that the country was at war, as well as the way the government had managed the war. She must have sensed my nervousness, because she told me that the average Iraqi soldier was not a threat. She mentioned that she and other members of her unit lived with the Iraqi soldiers on the camp. Both my eyes and ears were wide open as our conversation continued.

As a medic, Sergeant Law cared for both wounded American soldiers, and Iraqi prisoners. "The Iraqis lack the funding for training and materials. We were required to treat them, and I never had a problem working with the Iraqi soldiers." Again, she wanted me to know that I would be safe. "Treat people fairly. Those who look for trouble, always find trouble. Stay focused on the mission, and you should survive your tour okay." Her words were undoubtedly reassuring. I was grateful for meeting her, and she instantly became my heroine. I thanked her, by letting her know that I admired her courage and I was thankful for the time and information that she shared with me.

Sergeant Todd eventually showed up, and I shared everything that Sergeant Law shared with me, with him. He was from my home state. I was impressed at how knowledgeable Sergeant Todd was of all the training that we were going through. Even though he was 20 years younger, he seemed to understand me more than the others. He would always assist me with my shortcomings. We had been informed that we would be assigned to work together once we get to Iraq. Those were some of the reasons I chose him as my 'battle buddy.'

Sergeant Todd and I received word that the two of us were to attend a last-minute training session on communication equipment, along with a handful of other soldiers. This class was taught by a couple of civilian contractors. One from Australia, one from England, and a third one was a former U.S. marine. The entire military operation in Iraq involved a mix of coalition forces. Not only were soldiers from the NATO assisting with fighting, but they were also engaged with the training process.

The marine who nearly spent his whole career in the national guard, served as an officer. He had served two tours in Iraq already, and mentioned that his last tour was in 2004. He alluded to the fact that he was a member of the elite forces, and ended his career after serving sixteen years of military service. He said that his experience in Iraq caused him great stress and pain.

"I was not at all concerned about the four years that I had remaining to receive full retirement benefits. I wanted to stay alive. I've been wounded on two different occasions while serving in Iraq. I will never step another foot in that country." The former marine officer told us that is was the most dangerous place he had ever been. I was sort of forced to sit and listen to his spill about his dangerous encounters in Iraq. I didn't agree with the timing of his story.

I found nothing reassuring about what I was hearing from the former marine officer. We were days away from being deployed to the very same place he was speaking of. Although I sympathized with him, I would have been better off not hearing his story so close to my deployment. It was the total opposite of Sergeant Law's story one day earlier.

"I refuse to risk my life over policies that I did not believe in," was one of the last statements that the ex-marine said, before moving on with the training session.

His speech remained with me for the rest of the day, and it got me thinking all over again. I ended up second guessing if I wanted to take the risk. Why was the U.S. Government so preoccupied with the war in Iraq? Of course, like many other Americans, I thought I knew the real reason. But, I knew I wasn't going to be like the marine and just walk away from a career with only months left on my contract.

It wasn't easy, but my instincts told me to accept the advice that Sergeant Law gave me and move on. The marine's statement compounded the fact that everyone will encounter different experiences during their deployment.

To add to the mental confusion a meeting was held in the Post Chapel later that evening. The division commander, along with a few of his assistance commanders, called the meeting. Even though the meeting was held in the post chapel, it had nothing to do with religion. From my perspective, it was more of a pep rally. I always looked at a chapel as a sacred place to connect with one's spiritual self, or with one's God. On that occasion, it was used for neither.

There were so many soldiers present that it took several minutes before everyone was seated. On the stage was a large screen showing videos of soldiers already in Iraq. Images of fighter pilots on missions seeking out the enemy and blowing them to bits with their powerful missiles. Other videos showed soldiers celebrating their kill, or they're not being killed during battle. We watched IEDs blowing up military vehicles as convoys passed through villages. Similar to the training videos, with the rock music being blasted from the speakers that were set up on the stage. But this time it was inside the chapel.

I didn't think the post chapel was an appropriate place for that kind of proceeding. I had been a soldier for some time, and it's not like I had virgin ears, but I felt that the language the officers used was not suitable for a place of worship. To add icing on the cake, before it all ended, the chaplain led us in a word of prayer. Prayer, with weapons strapped to our bodies, swearing, videos, and rock music, my mind was completely twisted. I did not understand why a pep rally of that sort was held in a chapel.

The twenty-ninth of May was Memorial Day, and we were assembling once again, but it was not the sizable group that we had a few days earlier. The building was secured, and guards were placed on the outside. This gathering was a simulated military exercise, abbreviated as Simex. Because it was Memorial Day, one of the colonels was responsible for drafting up the training gave us a briefing about past and current events in Iraq. He had already visited Iraq participating in an exploratory exercise, before the departure of the unit.

The colonel spoke of a Noncommissioned Officer (NCO) who traveled along with him. He told us that the NCO was killed from the results of a blast from a roadside bomb. Once again, we received more disturbing news just days before we were to deploy.

"I'd like to have a moment of silence in honor of the NCO who recently lost his life," he said. Not going into more detail about the incident, he began his briefing on the unit's deployment mission.

Following the colonel's presentation, we were broken down into teams and possible sections that we would be working with while deployed. The exercise lasted for one week. We spent between nine and ten hours each day training before we were allowed to return to the barracks. Guards were left in place to ensure that none of the sensitive equipment was tampered with by anyone.

The commanding general of the division attended the daily briefings, and each day we had as many as three or four informal gatherings. What was said during the meetings was mostly confidential. But one subject the general talked about that was not confidential, was how to deal with the media if ever approached. Like other government agencies, the military had assigned personnel for that purpose. As a soldier, you were advised not to consent to an interview with the media. However, we were told if we found ourselves in a predicament, we should think first. As a service member, you waived certain rights of the First Amendment.

I was able to understand the reasoning behind that rule. If a soldier talked out of turn, they might unwittingly have a breach of security that could result in the loss of life. Everyone had their own story to tell, in this case there was the possibility of false information being rumored. I for one didn't want to talk to the media, in fear that I might say the wrong thing.

We even went as far as practicing simulated interviews, given soldiers some idea of how to respond, or how to manipulate the media, if there was ever a need. We practiced a series of scenarios, that would prepare us for dealing with propaganda. Overall, I think this Simex was necessary to introduce us to a more realistic approach to other possible encounters, other than combat. There is not a lot more I can reveal about the Simex being that many things we trained on were confidential. Three takeaways for me was the training on 'operating inside a mobile command post, conducting radio communications and map reading.'

The Simex training kept everyone busy as time was winding down. Although the training was still necessary, we reached a point where leaving became my main focus. Most did not talk about it, but I could feel the buildup of anxiety that surrounded me. To add to my distress, a day before we were to deploy; on June 5th, my daughter graduated from High School. I was sad that I could not be there. Nothing else was on my mind that day, not even my deployment. It was one of the most significant events of her life, and I was not present. I felt that I let her down as a father, but because of my deployment, and the required training, with no chance for makeup, I had to remain at Ft McCoy.

I was able to reach Annika on her cell phone moments after she walked across the stage. It meant a lot to hear her voice and to share her joy over the airwaves for just a few minutes. She understood the predicament I was in, and the reason I could not attend. Talking with her helped us both to feel better. Afterwards, I was able to go back to concentrating on my immediate future.

5

We were all done; training was complete; there was less than a week left before we were to leave Ft McCoy. Finally, the four-day pass was approved, according to the word of mouth that was going around the barracks. The final details were not precise, but still, everyone was excited. A majority of soldiers wanted to go home one more time before leaving for Iraq.

Colonel Sam made it clear that we could take a pass, starting on the 8th of June, and we must return on the 12th. It was not a lot of time to travel, especially for those who had to go a great distance. Given all the training we had been through in only a few short weeks, many of us felt that taking the trip was worth the risk.

I was excited about the opportunity to go home for the weekend. I needed a break and to spend one more weekend with my family. I had learned a great deal more about Iraq, and what to expect when I arrive. It was important for me to share the information with my family members, and to lift their spirits, as well as my own. During normal times it would have been ridiculous to travel so far and pay an excessive fee for a weekend trip. But those were not normal times. Despite all the hype, and Colonel Sam advising us that the pass was approved, some things were still not clear. The final yeah or nay, was in the hands of one man. Everyone was waiting for the headquarters commander back in Charlotte to make the decision.

The morale of the soldiers became an issue. It was impossible for anyone to make plans. I really didn't want to call my family and tell them that it's possible, I might be coming home on a four-day pass. I needed to wait to get more information. Throughout the day, pop up briefings were held to discuss the hot issue of the four-day pass. Some soldiers leaked the information out to their families, and things got serious. Family members got involved and were waiting for the final decision. For two days the issue whether the pass would be permitted was unresolved.

Time was running out and very few days were left before we were to deploy. Travel plans, if any, needed to be finalized for those of us who were planning to go home. Rumors were going around that we would be granted a pass with no cost. As a result of the rumors, questions came up over who would be responsible for paying each soldier's fair. Some soldiers felt the government should foot the bill. It would have been a nice thing for the government to do, but that suggestion was dead on arrival. Another idea came up that a plane should be chartered to fly everyone to a central location on each coast. That too didn't gain any traction.

A few soldiers took the matter to another level. They informed their spouses of what was going on, and things turned out to be not so good for the command. Several spouses contacted their congressional representatives over the morale issue in the unit. They alleged the leaders were losing control and not able to make modest decisions. Whatever the spouses said to the congressional representatives, must have worked. A meeting was called, within moments of hearing of the rumor. "Soldiers, I can assure you that this time your four-day pass had been approved. However, you must pay your own fare." Colonel Sam stood before us and said. The commanders tried to meet us halfway, by doing what they could to speed the process. We were allowed to begin travel a few hours earlier, because of the distances that some soldiers had to travel.

We rushed to find out information on departing flights from Minneapolis St. Paul airport. It is the largest airport in the region, but a distance away. We discovered a nearby smaller airport in Lacrosse, Wisconsin. Those of us who chose to make the trip found that airport to be more convenient. The government helped out as much as possible and provided a shuttle bus to the Lacrosse Airport twice a day, at no cost.

The next important call I made was to my family, informing them that I would be coming home. I wanted desperately to make the trip. When I finally found a flight, it came at a higher cost. The next dilemma that had to be resolved was catching a flight to Minneapolis. On a routine basis, a small plane is used to fly to Minneapolis, where all connections are made. The airport in Lacrosse got flooded with calls from soldiers trying to fly out. A decision was made to bring in a larger plane to support the mission. Again, prices went up as a result. We were willing to pay the cost. I was yearning to get home.

Hours later I made it home. The tireless effort that was put into making the trip paid off. I was one happy soldier. The first order of business was to fill in my family members on all that I had been through while at Fort McCoy. I was glad to be able to cuddle with my wife and to sleep in my bed again. Thekla and I took long walks while I updated her on my encounters at Fort McCoy. But, needless to say, those four days flew by. I was so very thankful for the opportunity to spend a few more days at home.

Then the time came to leave home again, and at that point, I felt like someone turned off my brightest light, without warning. My happiness turned into sadness as I returned to the airport. But despite the quick turnaround it was all worth it: the flight, cost, and even the turmoil.

I traveled back on the same route that brought me home. The four days turned into five. All the soldiers who went home were thankful for the extra travel day that was given. I got back to Fort McCoy around one o'clock in the morning, and I was completely drained, but again, thankful for the opportunity I had to go home.

With hardly any sleep, at four in the morning, my eyes were wide open. I took advantage of the quiet time. I needed a few personal moments to think before the crowd woke up, and all the confusion began. I spent one full day before departure, making last-minute adjustments, and looking over documents. I checked everything that I could think of before departure time.

Our team moved three times in one day. We moved out of the barracks that we had been in since arriving at Ft McCoy. Giving up my space was a real sign that we were at the end of our stay. Even though it was tense, we stuck together. The bond between a few of us grew even closer, as we faced an uncertain future.

June 17th was the eve of departure. Everything was expected to be in place. We had one final massive gathering in the post theater. The second in command, Colonel Woods, called the meeting, along with the division chaplain, and the battalion chaplain. All three were southern white males. Colonel Woods, from the western NC mountains, was the division chaplain. I felt like I was sitting in an old-fashioned southern big revival tent.

The purpose of the southern style church gathering was to allow the unit as a whole to come together one last time. Colonel Woods gave us an emotional testimony about his faith and how he intended on getting closer to his God while in Iraq. His testimony inspired others to give their testimony about their past, or just to ask for prayer. Many soldiers got emotional as they gave their testimonies. I was surprised that there were no considerations for the soldiers of other religions. The army has always been one of America's most prominent cultural melting pots, which lead me to believe that everyone would have been represented.

I had never witnessed anything like it before. Colonel Woods went as far as to predict that a small number of soldiers sitting in the audience would probably not return with us.

"What was he saying? Did he just put a curse on us?" Those were two questions I asked myself as I listened very attentively to what was being said. The chaplains started praying for victory in Iraq. This is where I got lost. I didn't understand. Once again, my mind was all twisted. I was not sure if we were going to raise hell, and kill a whole lot of people, or if we were going to save souls. Besides, why would they pray for victory instead of peace, I wondered. I felt that peace was needed more than violence, or victory. It was not my style of worship. We were talking about destroying people. Many of them were probably not much different than most of us in the audience. And not to forget the innocent people who would die as a result of our actions. I left the final pep rally more confused than I was when I went in.

****

The day of June 18th, 2006, will forever remain in my mind, it was the day of departure. I was up early that morning, rushing to make last minute phone calls. I called both of my brothers, and my father, to say goodbye. These were sobering phone calls. I wasn't sure when I would talk to either of them again. I could not bring myself around to calling my wife, calling her would be too difficult.

When I returned to the barracks, everyone was up and preparing for movement. Soon after the call was made for everyone to assemble in groups according to last names, all bags were moved across the street, to be loaded on cargo trucks. I had been a member of the red team for two months. After we assembled one last time in the waiting area, the teams were dismantled. That was the official ending of training at Ft Mc-Coy; we were moving forward.

We were ordered to a restricted section of a paved parking lot, were we were fenced in like cattle. We waited there for three hours before we boarded buses for the air hangars. They were located at an air national guard base some thirty miles away from Ft McCoy. When we arrived there, we were greeted by DOD Civilian employers who gave us strict guidelines to follow while waiting to board the plane. We had to go through a customs inspection, to ensure that no one was trying to smuggle any contraband out of the country.

The checks took about an hour before completion. Afterwards, I found a space to lay on the hard freshly painted concrete floor. I closed my eyes, but not to sleep. I spent the last few moments on the ground praying and meditating on what will or what was likely to happen in my future.

"Ladies and gentlemen, may I have your attention. I need everyone to take all your belongings and line up to begin boarding the plane."

This time I was in no rush. I walked slowly dreading to board the plane. I wanted to stay on the ground until the very last second. As I got closer to the plane, I looked up and saw one of the largest passenger planes ever. It was an Airbus, able to fit the whole unit. Once everyone was seated, the captain came across the PA system welcoming everyone with the routine pilot to passenger spiel. But, this pilot did something that wasn't routine. The captain took a moment out and prayed over the PA system for every one of us before taking off. After the last two pep rallies, this time I believed his prayers were welcomed by most.

Moments after the prayer, the giant aircraft accelerated down the runway, increasing speed and rising high above the scattered clouds, as phase one of our journey began.

We were in for a very long flight. Once we were airborne, I tried to get as comfortable as possible. The flight attendant had already announced that the first stop would be Ireland. All the crew members served us well. I could easily tell by their hospitality that we were indeed not the first group of soldiers that they hosted. I'm sure that they knew how most of us were feeling. There was an impressive selection of movies to choose from if we wanted a distraction. However, I passed on the movies. I was more interested in sleep and tracking the flight on the monitors periodically.

Hours had passed, and before we knew it, we were preparing for landing in Ireland. I had flown to Europe many times, but this was my first stop in Ireland. From the passenger window, I was able to see the dark green countryside. I had the perfect view to watch the fog slowly rise from the hills, opening a picture of one of nature's spectacular landscapes, before the plane landed on the ground. The countryside was beautiful.

We walked off the plane for a break and were permitted to mingle in the duty shops of the terminal. I am not able to recall the town or the airport, but the airport terminal was smaller than what I anticipated. But before taking a stroll around the terminal, I rushed to freshen up and take a few moments to stretch. It was only a matter of time before I would find myself crammed back into my seat on the plane.

Standing not far away from the gate waiting for the call to reload, I looked through the large glass plated windows, and scanned over the wet countryside, daydreaming. It didn't dawn on me right away, that was to be the last rainfall I would see for more than five months. Then came the call to reload the plane. I took my seat feeling a little fresher, both physically and mentally. But, as soon as we were airborne; moments later I was fast asleep.

I was exhausted from the anxiety and my sleepless last night back in the States. Leaving had been the only thing on my mind. Even though I had two and a half months to prepare for the journey, when the time came to leave, I still was not prepared. For me, the thought of going off to war was out of the ordinary. I don't think anyone could have prepared themselves for the journey, regardless of the amount of training that they had received.

The sleep I got on the plane was much needed. The next time I woke up, I looked at the monitor tracking the flight. I saw that we were getting closer to Kuwait. The plane had entered the airspace of the Middle East. I could see the city of Baghdad was still a distance away. Okay, I thought, you're almost there, and it's impossible to turn around, no need to look back.

Then I whispered a prayer. My prayer was simple. I prayed for my safekeeping, as well as the safekeeping for us all. I prayed that I would be strong and do the very best that I could. I asked my God to help me always keep a positive attitude, and stay focused. From that point on, everything was out of my hands. I no longer had control of my destiny. There wasn't anything left to do but face the challenges that were ahead.

The tracking screen showed that we were just over 100 kilometers from Kuwait. I was nervous and wished for the butterflies in my stomach to fly away. I looked out of the window, and saw the never-ending desert, with massive oil fields in every direction. Then I started thinking: it's no coincidence, it's all related. The oil fields, that's why we are here. It's for the oil. But no, the President of the United States had said, "The purpose of the mission is to liberate the Iraqi people from a dictatorship."

I have debated that issue over and over again in my mind. Doing so at the moment when we were about to land was not the time to do it again. I was already far into a position that nothing could change. All at once, like a stage curtain let down; darkness fell. An enormous sea of metropolitan lights became visible.

6

The pilot began to make his final announcement, I along with several other passengers suddenly placed our hands over our ears as a powerful electrical charge of static blasted through the PA system. "Ladies and Gentlemen, I would like to announce that we are coming up on our destination. Within minutes we will be landing in Kuwait City. On behalf of Royal Airlines, I wish you all Godspeed."

The plane landed in Kuwait, at Kuwait City International Airport on June 19th, at 2205 Arabic Standard Time (AST). A US Army representative boarded the plane and welcomed us to Kuwait. He gave instructions on what we were to do once we were off the plane.

"I need a few soldiers to assist with loading the baggage onto the trucks, and everyone else should load up on the buses to my left."

The buses would take us to Camp Buehring, about 30 kilometers away. Once we were seated, a young female air force sergeant, stepped on the bus giving us additional information that we would need when we arrived onto the camp.

"Do not open the curtains, they are there for security reasons," she said, before stepping off the bus. The bus eased off and began the journey to Camp Buehring. A curtain was dangling in the window on my left. The sergeant's statement about not opening the curtains increased my curiosity about what the outside looked like.

The bus was being driven by a dark-skinned man with a thick black mustache. He wore a maroon turban and concentrated on his driving without uttering one word. Except for a few whispered conversations, it was relatively quiet on the bus. I was exhausted, but my curiosity kept me awake. The driver pulled the bus over at a rest stop for a short break. Stepping off the bus, I was greeted by a warm breeze and blowing sand. I remember feeling the heat of the pavement through the soles of my boots.

When I turned to step back on the bus, I recognized that the bus was being escorted by military police, in tactical vehicles. Their presence increased my wanting to know about the outside. Within minutes of being back on the road, I took my chances. Finally, I broke the rules, by doing what I was told not to do. I opened the curtain just enough for a quick peek out. The moon was bright and provided enough light that I was able to see only a small fraction of the endless desert.

The farther the bus traveled, the less smooth the ride became. Some twenty or thirty minutes later, we came upon several bright lights. The lights were powered by small generators, those that you usually see being used at road construction sites. They were spaced equally apart for several hundred meters. The lights enable the security guards to see anyone or anything that approached the heavily guarded gate.

The guards who greeted us at the entrance were all civilians, wearing black short-sleeved polo shirts, tan khaki pants, and matching brown desert boots. One of the guards with a short military crew cut entered the bus. He did not speak one word, but simply strutted down the aisle with his chest out, and his weapon visible, as to demonstrate that he was the guy in charge. Later I would find out that they were contractors who worked for the former infamous Blackwater Security.

After stepping off the bus, he turned in a very orderly manner and waved for the driver to proceed through the gate. As the driver drove the bus farther inside the camp, we approached rows of tents on both sides of the road. The tents and the few buildings had the likeness of a small town out in the middle of the desert. It was almost midnight when we arrived. There were small groups of soldiers out jogging. Others were walking around as if it was the middle of the day.

The bus stopped in front of one of the designated tents, in an area where we would be spending the next few days. Once off the bus, we gathered into a large formation and again were greeted by a representative, who gave more instructions.

"Welcome to Camp Buehring, you will be here for the next few days processing and to become acclimatized to the Middle East. I need to collect and scan everyone's ID cards."

We all gave up our ID cards to begin processing. The clerk only had the ID cards for a few moments and scanned them into a system that would account for each service member being physically present in the Middle East. I suppose that the chip on ID cards had some sort of tracking device that could determine a service members location. Which was a good thing if you found yourself in trouble. On the other hand, you might not have felt too comfortable knowing that big brother was always watching.

Someone shouted out the order, "Move inside the briefing tent, and take a seat in one of the metal chairs in front of the podium." While inside we were given a short welcoming briefing to Camp Buehring. We were also assigned sleeping quarters inside one of the large white tents, a few tents down from the operations tent.

As many as thirty soldiers were assigned to one tent. Having that many soldiers assigned to one tent; resulted in very tight sleeping conditions. Sleeping cots were lined up on both sides of the interior lining of the tent. We were sleeping with less than three feet separating us. Thank God, for the large air conditioning units on both sides of the tent; otherwise, we would have not survived.

We were required to attend two mandatory short classes during our first two days at the camp. The first class was weapons training at the range, and the other was general information we should know, before moving into Iraq. It was half past midnight before we were released either to go to chow or go to bed. I chose to grab a bite to eat before going to bed. Like the other soldiers, I was wide awake.

Entering into a different time zone had a considerable effect on my body. No one was able to sleep, because of the eight-hour difference between Kuwait City and Ft McCoy. We all were experiencing some sort of jet lag. It seemed like everyone ended up in the dining hall, catching midnight chow, before closing.

With little sleep, morning arrived too soon. It was about 6:30 AM when I walked outside of the tent to go to the mobile toilets. "OH MY GOD!" I was not ready for what I experienced. The temperature was already over 100 degrees Fahrenheit. It was unbelievably hot, for so early in the morning, and the sun was so high and bright that I was practically blinded without sunglasses. I could only stay outside of the tent for a short moment. I felt like I was walking in a sauna. I rushed back inside the tent, only to experience a temperature of nearly 90 degrees. With only two of the four large air conditioners working, it felt very uncomfortable inside the tent.

Sleeping next to me was Sergeant H. He was one of the most contentious soldiers I met during my deployment. He woke up complaining about the conditions in the tent. It took me a while to get used to Sergeant H's constant complaints. Since the day I met him back at Fort McCoy, he complained about everything. However, this time his complaint was justifiable. Not only was the heat unbearable in the tent, but ants were crawling all over our bags. We had to check all our items, piece by piece to get rid of the ants.

Sergeant H. and I took a break and went for breakfast. We didn't miss a meal, because that was one of the highlights of our day. We stepped out of the tent this time experiencing the heat along with a light sand storm. I thought I was prepared this time, by wearing sunglasses. The sunglasses were of little help. I still felt like I was walking head-on into a large bright light, and forced to feel my way along. I used my hands to protect my face from the small pebbles of sand that were blowing around.

"How are we going to survive these unbearable conditions for a year?' Sergeant H. asked as we struggled to get to the chow tent.

A couple of hours after breakfast, we completed the first class. We had no more commitments for the rest of the day. Later in the afternoon, a mandatory formation for accountability was held. We could spend the rest of the day as we pleased while trying to acclimatize to our new environment.

On our second day in Kuwait, we were awoken at 0200 a.m. Then we departed for the firing range. We were told that the earlier we left, the less time we would have to spend out in the heat. We were on the buses for almost forty-five minutes, riding across the Kuwaiti desert, this time there were no curtains. The sites of the wide-ranging desert were the core focus of my attention. Somewhere near 0400 hours in the morning, we had arrived at the ranges and were rushed to line up for test firing of our weapons.

It was hard for me to concentrate on what the instructors were saying. I was mesmerized by the sun rising in the Kuwaiti desert, at such an early hour. It was indeed one of the most amazing views that my eyes have ever witnessed. I was able to block out all the sounds and concentrate only on the sunrise. The sun appeared from behind a distant large mound of sand. It was a solid bright color of orange. It wasn't easy to see, but I managed to glance at the flaming ring of fire that encircled it. It was huge and moving upward at a steady pace. It's orange and yellow colors mixed well with vast plains of the desert. The imagines of the sunrise will forever remain in my memory.

Eventually, the sound of gunfire brought me back to reality. It was getting close to my turn to fire my M4 rifle. I shot off the forty rounds that were issued to me without any problems. During that round of firing of weapons, there was no recording on how well we did; it was only a familiarization firing. When everyone had completed, we reloaded the buses and returned back to Camp Buehring.

Once we arrived back at the camp, Sergeant H and I decided to walk around and check out the place. We certainly did not want to spend the rest of the day inside the hot tent. We walked around the camp for a while, trying to locate a more relaxed spot. That's when we discovered a makeshift internet café, inside a medium size tent. It was a great discovery. I remember it was from there that I was able to send my first email from the Middle East to my family, giving them an update on my whereabouts. Sending that email was a relief. It took some of the weight off my shoulders. I knew the importance of staying in touch with loved ones. It was vital to my survival. When I knew things were good at home, it made things a lot easier for me.

I was surprised to meet a young American woman, from New Jersey, who worked in the Morale, Welfare, and Recreation Center. For weeks we had been told that the region was too dangerous for civilians and there was a great deal of training that needed to be completed before going. On account of everything that we had been told, I was surprised to have run into this young lady.

If I had to guess the age of the young lady from New Jersey, I would say she was around twenty-three. She worked for a private contractor as a recreation coordinator. The young lady invited Sergeant H. and myself inside the medium size, sand-colored, rectangle military tent. She was busy organizing a few things, but she did ask the two of us to come inside and to take a seat at a round game table. She designed the tent to be a recreational area for the soldiers on the camp. The tent included a

TV, books, magazines, and many small items of interests that were sent by mail from the U.S. to entertain the troops. Most important was the online computers, enabling soldiers to send and receive emails.

For most of the afternoon, in between her duties, she would stop and conversate with us. Her subjects were interesting and informative. She really put my mind at ease after I had heard nothing but negative reports coming out of the Middle East. "I enjoy living abroad, and the fact that I can live with my husband on the local economy," she said.

Camp Buehring was her husband's assigned duty station while he was in the Middle East. She said she commuted to work alone each day while driving nearly 30 minutes one way through the desert. That was shocking information from my point of view.

"Yes, I suppose it is dangerous, but I try not to think about it. I disguise my identity of being an American as much as I can."

Disguising herself couldn't have been easy. The young lady was about five feet, two inches, light complexion, and with shoulder length blonde hair. All the local females that I saw during my short stay in Kuwait had either a light or dark brown complexion, with thick black hair, or wore hijabs.

It was a real pleasure meeting and spending time with this young woman. Her simple class of mixing in with the local culture was more interesting than the previous official classes I'd attended.

After little sleep, I woke up to another hot morning and still at Camp Buehring. It was useless trying to sleep in a super-hot tent. Truthfully, I don't think anyone was able to sleep. Soldiers walked in and out of the tent, after tossing and turning all night, with no luck sleeping, I decided to end my misery and get up as well.

There was no change in the weather, it seemed, even more, hotter than the day before. I got dressed and walked to breakfast alone; I was fortunate that the sand was not blowing. The walk allowed me a few moments of meditation. I desperately needed to adjust my attitude, after sleeping next to one of the most negative soldiers on the team. I didn't want any of his misfortunes to rub off on me. With the situation as bad as it was, I did my best to avoid anyone in the group, who gave off negative vibes. Even though he slept only three feet from me; thank God that the situation was only temporary.

The lone walk to breakfast was an enjoyable experience. There wasn't much to see, but several bright white tents one after the other. It was one of the few moments of solitude that I was able to find. It all changed when I walked into the dining tent. The noise level intensified, and I was suddenly surrounded by the many soldiers who already filled the tent.

I had no complaints about the meal. The dining staff did an excellent job of pleasing everyone who entered. They served just about anything one might want to have for breakfast. We were given as many bottles of water and Gatorade that we were able to carry. That was one of the ways of ensuring that every- one remained hydrated, while out in the sweltering heat.

Not only were the drinks distributed in the dining facilities, but they were also placed throughout the tents, and along with many sorrel bags of ice placed throughout the camp. It did not take me long to understand the importance of both Gatorade and the sorrel bags of ice. Equally important were the air condi- tioners. No one could survive a night in the high temperatures without neither.

Whether just laying around trying to get some rest, in the male tents we stripped down to our underwear, without covers, trying to stay cool while sleeping. Some decided not to sleep at all, and sat outside the tent most of the night, smoking cigarettes and holding conversations. Not that it was cooler outside, but they were trying to cope with their insomnia.

7

On the 21st day of June, immediately after breakfast, we were told to prepare to board one of the buses waiting outside of the dining area. Our unit was scheduled to be issued additional personal combat gear for use in Iraq. One of the staff members said, "Soldiers the bus ride will be just under an hour."

We left for the outpost some 50 kilometers away. I positioned myself on the very first seat to the right side of the driver. I wanted to be able to check out the view from the large windows up front. The windows provided a great panorama view of the desert settings.

I have been fortunate in my life, and I have seen some of the world's most marveling cities, but never have I seen anything like the bareness of the Kuwaiti desert. It was a once in a lifetime adventure. All the while I was thinking about what to expect while deployed, it never crossed my mind that I would travel through the Kuwaiti desert.

The road was formed from the remnants of the hard-compressed sand, which caused it to be rough and bumpy at times. A slightly fresh coat of blowing sand, covering all the tracks, left me wondering if many vehicles even traveled the route at all. An air force officer who was familiar with the road, told us "The sandstorms occur almost daily here making it difficult to see the highway. Only a skillful driver can find their way through the blowing sand." I did notice that there were international road markers posted on both sides of the highway.

Still, I was amazed by how well the driver navigated the oversize bus across the desert without wandering off the course. I suppose the markers were useful tools in helping the driver navigate his way. As the bus traveled farther down the road, the sand ceased to blow, just in time for everyone to focus on a distance view out on the horizon. What we all were seeing, appeared to be a dark configuration of movement. As the bus got closer, I saw it was life: it was a herd of wild camels standing near the roadway. No one on the bus uttered a word. The only sounds that I could hear were cameras clicking simultaneously. Almost everyone on the bus was trying to capture photos of one of nature's wonders.

Continuing down the highway, there were more camels. This time a man was standing nearby with two dogs, as he appeared to be watching over the herd. He was the lone soul, standing there with his animals. There appeared to be no other structures nearby, and it looked like the man had constructed a temporary canvass to protect himself from the hot sun. I was curious about how far the man traveled, being that there was nothing else close by.

Further down the highway, there were scattered piles of trash. The trash piles looked as if they had been purposely dumped, turning that stretch of the desert into a miniature landfill. The next thing I observed was a camel corpse lying meters from the road out in the open desert.

Dead camels were not the most baffling thing that I saw. It was even more mysterious seeing a man walking out across the scorching desert all alone. I saw nothing or no one else close by. He was wearing a headscarf, a long-sleeved shirt, and wide baggy pants. I assumed his choice of light-colored clothing was to provide him protection from the sizzling sun. It was surprising to me. I only saw him, the lone wanderer, walking across no man's land. I couldn't help but wonder where he came from, and where was he going. Watching him walking through no man's land left me with a sense of wonder.

The driver reduced the speed of the bus as we approached the gate of the remote military camp. The entrance was guarded by two men with an insignia on the right side of their black polo shirts that read, "Blackwater Security." This time neither of them entered the bus. One of the guards stepped out from the nearby guard shack, without any look of concern on his face. He walked over to the driver's side of the bus, where the driver flipped open a small window. The two men exchanged a few brief words, and then he waved the driver through the gates.

After stepping off the bus into the bright sunshine and extreme heat, it took a couple of moments before I was able to pull myself together. Everyone formed into a line before walking towards a large sandy beige metal building that stood isolated across the gravel parking lot. Inside were several cages with large cardboard boxes filled with equipment. The first pieces of equipment that we received was the individual body armor vest (IBA), nicknamed "Battle Rattle."

Regardless of the temperature outside, it was mandatory that we wear the gear at all times unless cleared by the commander. The extra gear amounted to an additional 20 or 25 pounds of extra weight to carry, along with a rifle and a smaller handgun on your hip. The weight did not include the backpacks. Together the total weight ended up being somewhere around 35 to 45 pounds. "That's okay," said one of the army's staff members. The gear was supposed to be lighter than the gear we trained with. "It's new and improved," the staff member sarcastically yelled out.

Another staff member gave a small spill about the 'Battle Rattle' gear and how it was designed to save lives. I bought into his logic. I said, if it saves lives, then it's worth getting used too. I had no further comments.

Both young and old soldiers alike were huffing and puffing as we struggled to walk across the hot gravel parking lot. The additional weight had an impact on everyone. Walking back to the cool buses wasn't as easy. Fortunately, we didn't have to wear the equipment right away. We placed the newly issued equipment underneath the coaches in the cargo compartment. I was happy to reload the bus escaping the high temperatures and to relax in the comfort of the air conditioning. We waited for hours before everyone was done receiving all of their equipment.

"Soldiers, we have a problem," a staff member announced. The problem was with the drivers. We were informed that the drivers were not allowed to work beyond their scheduled eight-hour shift. The drivers had reached their time limit during the wait. No fault of their own, but it took longer than expected for every soldier to be served.

A replacement for the drivers had to be called out to take us back to the main military camp in Kuwait. We later discovered that it was only part of the problem. All the gear had to be taken off the buses and loaded onto replacement buses. With the temperature, sizzling around 120-degrees it wasn't easy.

As soon as all unloading and reloading of the gear was completed, another major issue became apparent. With all the moving around and shifting of equipment, two soldiers reported that their weapons were missing. Now we had ourselves a real problem. One that could create even more problems for whoever was responsible for the weapons. We spent over 45 minutes matching up serial numbers and trying to locate the missing weapons.

Foreign workers were interacting around us for most of the day. No one wanted to falsely accuse anyone, but being that we had recently arrived in the Middle East and hearing rumors of terrorism, many were starting to speculate, what if? I was included in the group of soldiers who were suspicious of the drivers and the possibility of one of them stealing the weapons.

I made the mistake of prejudging others, based on the opinions of others. Never mind the fact that I always tried to practice not judging anyone based on their looks or religious belief.

But thank God, the missing weapons were finally found. That brought an end to the miserable moment's everyone spent searching for them. Finding the weapons did not end all of the speculation about the foreign workers. There were a few soldiers in the group who would never let up on their prejudices of the local people and Muslims.

We finally began the trip back to Camp Buehring. The adventurous road journey that we started out on ended up being a lot of work, some ten hours later. The spectacular sites of the desert eventually calmed everyone on the bus back down. Those who weren't sleeping were on the lookout for more sights of nature's wonders.

Looking out the window to my right, I got a glimpse of a single structure located a few meters into the desert, perhaps a farmhouse standing alone. There was not a single tree anywhere near. I could not imagine anyone living in such an isolated place, where it was so hot and dry without adequate resources around. Further down I spotted a man standing nearby under a simple man-made roof.

The bus drove back by the Air Force camp that stood alone out in the middle of the desert as well. There were a few airmen out jogging down the road. I hoped there was no chance of me spending a year at a remote facility like that one. I was not sure if I would have survived it. Of course, at the time of the trip, I had no clue of where, or how I would be living, but I prayed it was better than what I was seeing.

Back at Camp Buehring, the word came down that evening that we would be leaving sooner than we anticipated. Everyone was told to go to the tents and pack their bags and prepare for departure around midnight. Again, we took buses from Camp Buehring to a staging area, that turned out to be the same air force camp where we received the additional training gear earlier that day. When we arrived at the camp, I was feeling a little anxious about Iraq. There wasn't too much good news coming out of that country.

Nightfall came quickly, and the landscape was well illuminated from the high beam security lanterns that were placed short distances apart inside the wire. From not far away, I could hear the sound of large engines roaring. Turning and looking in that direction, I saw a sizeable C-5 Galaxy cargo and troop carrier plane, idling its engines. The crew had just completed loading everyone's bags.

One of the platoon leaders mustered everyone together, moments before we would leave for Baghdad. He wanted to have one last prayer together before we loaded the plane.

At the end of the group prayer, we formed a single line to walk towards the aircraft, two soldiers in charge of the ammunition popped open a box, as we walked past them. They handed each one of us two 40 round magazines of bullets. They also gave an additional one 45 round magazine to every soldier for their nine-millimeter handguns.

We were not preparing for a training exercise, it was 'the real deal; It was time to rock and roll. ' The ammunition added more weight to the already heavy Battle Rattle gear that we were wearing. After receiving more ammunition, we were really huffing and puffing. Wearing and carrying all that extra weight was going to take some time getting used too.

Okay, I uttered to myself, not really knowing what to do next. Things were happening and happening fast. "Now is the time to visit the toilets, if you must, if not then we will commence boarding the C-5," the senior airman yelled out.

Still, in a single file, we walked up the back ramp, and entered the plane. One by one we began to fill the rows of seats. Because we were wearing the armor vest, headgear, and holding our rifles in our hands, we were hardly able to fit into the seats. This was the most uncomfortable seating arrangement that I ever had on a plane. I sat straight up with no room to move in either direction. We were squeezed in like sardines in a can. I sat in the center of five seats to a row. With sweat dripping down my face, I thought for sure I would suffocate before ever reaching Baghdad's International Airport.

After the crew chief finished his briefing, we were airborne again. I placed earplugs in my ears, hoping to get some sleep before the plane landed. But it was much too hot and too uncomfortable. I glanced at a digital timer on the wall and saw that the time was 0630. We had been up most of the night preparing for the flight to Iraq.

Luckily the trip was not that long, and exactly one hour later, we were preparing to land in Baghdad. It was not safe for the plane to make a normal landing. The pilot announced that he would be performing a spiral landing. This maneuver was designed to protect the plane from being hit by enemy fire. It took a little longer, however, there were no complaints because the landing was successful. Finally, we were on the ground in Baghdad. Not surprisingly, there were no cheers of celebration. The plane came to a halt, and we marched off. Exiting from the rear on the cargo ramp, I thanked God that the flight was over and I was able to move my body again.

We stood there directly in the morning sun, which was unbearable even at that time of day. Standing in full combat gear suffering from the heat while waiting for instructions, caused some soldiers to become disoriented. One soldier fainted, and minutes later two more soldiers passed out from heat exhaustion, just barley collapsing to the ground, before being caught by the soldiers standing nearby. Some ten minutes later, a sergeant from inside the tent walked out.

"It's okay to ground your combat gear, and move inside the tent," the sergeant said and waving his hand for everyone to enter. Once inside we began another round of processing information and we received our assignments for the next year.

I was assigned to work in the Green Zone. I knew nothing about Iraq, but I had heard that there was always activity in the

Green Zone. I made a request to be reassigned. Besides Sergeant Todd, and I was told that we would be working together. Colonel Sam took care of the matter, and my assignment was changed. My new assignment was Camp Taji, Iraq. I knew nothing about the place. I was told it was approximately 25 kilometers north of Baghdad.

"Okay guys that's it," yelled out another staff member. He told us to go back outside, gather our bags, and get onto one of the small blue-white shuttle buses parked to the left of the tent. The bus would take us to a resting place until we were able to be transported to Camp Taji.

The unit was being broken down into individual teams, averaging three to six soldiers per team. At that time, it was confirmed, I was being assigned to Camp Taji. Soldiers from the division were reassigned to different outposts all over the country. There were different modes of transport used to transport everyone to each camp. The majority would be flying by helicopter, and the others would travel in military convoys.

I sat on the shuttle bus with no working air condition, wearing the full 'battle rattle' gear for almost thirty minutes. I was drenched in sweat from sitting only. I stood up to go back inside the tent when Sergeant Todd, along with two more soldiers, and the driver finally showed up.

The driver drove the bus around the corner through a few narrow dusty and bumpy roads. Along the route stood tall concrete pillars, and razor wire fences encircling the compound. I could see large gashes in the walls, appearing to be scarring from some type of explosive munitions.

The small bus only drove for about 10 minutes before stopping in a gravel parking lot in front of rows and rows of tents. This was Camp Striker. We were supposed to spend the night there, with the hope of getting transportation to Camp Taji the following day. Many of the tents were worn and looked pretty bad. Sergeant Todd and I probably went through them all until we found one that we thought to be reasonably acceptable. The interior of the tent was okay, with only a few sleeping cots and a portable air conditioner, as well as a plywood floor, to keep the dust down.

Camp Striker was not the best place to stay, but it was better than sleeping out in the middle of the desert. Nearby were toilet trailers with showers. Depending on the time of day, determine whether the showers were warm or cold. No, it wasn't like home, but at least we had showers. Looking at it from a different perspective, we were lucky to have the facilities nearby the sleeping tents. We could have ended up walking a lot farther just to take a shower.

Before we were allowed time for a shower, we had to go back out in the heat and unload the trucks with all the baggage. The contract truck drivers were in a hurry to drop us off and leave. Some of the guys really started to complain. They said that it was too hot for unloading the trucks and that they had reached their limit. Sergeant H was leading the protest against working in the heat. "If the drivers are in such a hurry, maybe they should unload their own truck." He's right again, I thought.

The whole group became physically exhausted and frustrated from the lack of sleep. Without having food and little water, our bodies were slowly being worn down. Suddenly, Colonel Sam stood up with sweat rolling down his red puffy cheeks, and said, "That's it guys, I have had it. We're stopping. This time the drivers just have to wait."

Colonel Sam gave everyone an order to go get food and water, as well as rest. He did not say it a moment too soon. Everyone immediately stopped working and sped towards the dining tent.

We were only in Baghdad for a few hours, and things were not going well. After a meal and a short break, we finished unloading the luggage and we were finally able to get a shower. We ended up in the warm tents, making it difficult to fall asleep. It was after 0200 before it cooled down enough to sleep.

With just under four hours of sleep, we were awoken by the sounds of gunfire. Everyone sat up on their sleeping carts simultaneously. The noise was loud and coming from not more than 100 meters away; it was right on the other side of the concrete pillars. It was not a dream. With rifles in our hands, we just sat there looking at each other.

No one knew how to respond. It was our first morning in Iraq. I squeezed my rifle and started praying for protection. It was like being in a nightmare, but only everyone was awake and experiencing the same thing.

The gun battle lasted close to an hour. We got the news that the 101st Airborne Division had battled a group of insurgents, and it took place right on the other side of the concrete pillar, near our tent. Word quickly got around that two American soldiers were killed.

It took some time to digest all that had happened. Not even 24 hours in Iraq, and my life was in more danger than I realized. It was only the beginning. All the military training that I ever received throughout my career did not prepare me for my first morning in Iraq.

8

It wasn't long before things were calm again. We were informed we could use the day for some needed rest and recovery. It was a new day indeed, but nearly impossible not to think about the gun battle that happened a few hours earlier. Putting that incident aside, the camp appeared to be a secure place. I prayed that I would never wake up to another morning of such turmoil.

Rather than lay around all day, I decided to spend my first day in Iraq wandering around Camp Liberty. The gunfight helped me to realize the importance of wearing the battle rattle gear and carrying my weapon with me at all times. As odd as it might seem, we even had to carry our weapons to the shower. Never mind it was only a few yards from the tent. I wasn't exactly sure if I was prepared to participate in a firefight, but I knew at any moment a gunfight could become a reality. I knew I would have to always be prepared for the worst.

While roaming around the camp, I learned that there was a lot of history on Camp Liberty. It definitely would have taken more than one day to discover it all. I discovered that way back in former times, the camp had been occupied by an Iranian military group. The Iranian occupation took place long before the war between the two countries. When the American forces invaded Iraq in 2003, Camp Hurriya, which in Arabic means 'Freedom,' was renamed Camp Liberty. I guess the name kind of goes along with the mission. It's likely the name made it easier for the soldiers to pronounce. I speculate the name was also more patriotic and appealing to the occupying forces.

During one period after the second invasion in March 2003, the American soldiers were welcomed as "Liberators of freedom." This was all before the Country was ruined by the spread of fighting in nearly every major city in Iraq. This all took place in just a few years. The Shia majority no longer welcomed the American forces, after 10,000 of Iraqis were killed, including innocent women and children.

Speaking to different soldiers that I met along the way, I learned that the camp was larger than what I was able to see. A couple of soldiers standing by a bus stop informed me that I could take a shuttle bus to connect to two other camps, 'Camp Striker, and Camp Victory.' The entire compound was surprisingly huge, considering it was located in the middle of Baghdad.

I hopped on a shuttle bus, taking a ride up to one of the many palaces from which Saddam Hussein, the former leader of Iraq, ruled from. Considering all the stops in between the starting point, the trip turned out to be about a twenty-minute ride. By no means was it a luxury tour. The roads were dusty, and the shuttle buses air-conditioning was not working. There were only three people aboard the bus: myself, one other soldier, and an Iraqi civilian. A few windows were down, causing the interior of the bus to be filled with dust. I ruined my nice clean uniform by just taking a seat on the bus.

The roads had several large potholes all along the way, causing the ride to be rough and extremely bumpy. They had been partially destroyed from the heavy tactical military vehicles, and the heavy downpour of rain in the winter, I was told. I noticed some areas of vegetation along the way, with patches of tall desert weeds and dried up palm trees.

As the bus got closer, I was able to see two palaces high on a hill. The closer we got the vegetation grew thicker. There was a large body of water flowing from the Tigris river into a manmade lake, which was responsible for the growth of weeds. As the bus began to make its journey up the hill, there stood two small identical stone buildings on both sides of the road.

The Iraqi civilian on the bus who spoke English must have noticed how interested I was and wanted me to know that the buildings once housed Saddam Hussein's personal guards. "Most of the informal business was conducted in those buildings," he said.

High on a hill, were two large twin Palaces constructed from large blocks of stone. Both appeared to be stylish in design and were probably well maintained before the war. One of them showed signs of light damage. Tours inside both palaces were not allowed due to restricted access. I could only imagine what the insides must have looked like.

Never mind that I was not able to go inside neither Palace, the trip was worth it, if only to stroll the grounds. Besides, I was trying to pass time. I only spent less than an hour outside, because the heat started having an effect on me. I had not yet adapted to the high temperatures, and desperately needed a place to cool off. Catching the next shuttle down the hill, I made my way back to the tent, which was slightly cooler.

All night long I could hear the crunching sound of gravel as soldiers who were deprived of sleep, walked by the tents. I looked forward to getting up the next morning in order to move out of that warm and unwelcoming tent.

"Everyone going to Camp Taji should start moving. Pack your bags, there is a flight leaving for Camp Taji in a couple of hours," one of the staff members walked through the tent and shouted. This time it didn't take long to pack. Sergeant Todd and I collected our luggage and carried it over to the makeshift passenger terminal. Camp Taji is located 27km from Camp Liberty. We were flying out on a helicopter, which was said to be safer and more convenient. The terminal was located a few yards across from the Baghdad International Airport (BIAP).

The terminal operations were in an old dark army green canvas tent with plywood floors, that had been constructed by the U.S. military coalition. The thick canvas tent was nothing more than a dust collector in my eyes. I should not have complained about the conditions of the tent. Although it was a makeshift tent, it was air-conditioned, and it provided protection from the scorching sun. In addition, the operations were quite effective.

"You guys will be flown out to the middle of nowhere, and I wouldn't want to be in your shoes for the next year," a young sergeant who worked as a processing clerk, said with a smirk on his face. Instead of speaking words of encouragement, or wishing us well, he was sarcastic about our assignment.

Seven hours later our flight finally became available. We boarded the large and loud chinook helicopter that would take us to Camp Taji. The engine and rotors were so loud that the crew chief could only demonstrate his safety briefing by using his hands. I was very thankful for the earplugs that he passed out. At least the chinook helicopter was able to accommodate everyone without being shoehorned in.

It was close to midnight before we departed the Baghdad International Airport operation center. We were only in the air for about twenty minutes before landing at Camp Taji. It was sooner than I expected. The camp was a major hub for military helicopters, and it was once alleged to have been used by the Iraqi military to manufacture chemical weapons. That news blew me away. I was certain that residue from chemicals continued to linger in the ground. The helicopter came to a halt and the pilot turned off the engines, which enabled me to regain my hearing.

Colonel Sam, Sergeant Todd, and I, as well as other soldiers who were assigned to Camp Taji, were greeted by a young Air Force sergeant. As we all unloaded, we were given a short briefing. It seemed that we had more briefings in one business day than most normal operations have in a month. The sergeant wanted to go over a few rules, and what we should expect during the first week on the camp. Also included were more safety briefings, which for me, there could never have been enough. The sergeant continued to provide information on mandatory classes, uniforms, and places that were off limits.

We found ourselves unloading baggage at 0130 in the morning, with the temperature being around 90 degrees. It felt like we were performing hard labor. We were carrying and dragging luggage in the dark. Most of the luggage was just thrown into one large pile. We only took out what was necessary, since we were not able to find much in the dark.

Everyone was exhausted, tempers were flaring, and some guys started losing self-control. The welcoming staff saw that we were falling apart, and so they decided to dismiss everyone until daylight.

After a few hours of sleep, we were back up at 0600, starting all over again, gathering our luggage. With little sleep, there were a lot of grumpy soldiers at the breakfast tables on our first morning at the camp. They were boosted on, by Sergeant H. who acted as their leader.

We ended up in an area known as the Phoenix Academy, which was an Iraqi military camp. It was divided between the coalition soldiers and the Iraqi military. The academy was a smaller camp within a camp. Only authorized personnel were permitted to enter. We were required to remain at the academy for five days for more training classes. While there we would be retrained on the same training that we received at Fort McCoy. One doctrine the Army believes in, and it has proven to work, is repetitious training. Our first day of classroom training was meaningless because no one could stay awake long enough to grasp the information that was being given. Finally, the instructors realized this and canceled all training until the next day.

Day two, everyone returned to training refreshed and ready. The first thing that was discussed was more information on improvised explosive devices. According to the instructor, thirty percent of all deaths that had occurred were caused by IEDs.

The Pentagon had invested millions of dollars into research looking for a solution to prevent soldiers from being killed by these devices. Almost daily, the lives of Americans soldiers were put in danger as a result of IEDs being placed along the roadways. I had no problems staying awake for this particular lecture, even without properly working air conditioners or little sleep. Being taught how to stay alive was enough to keep me alert.

As the week continued we had additional classes in culture training. It was most important that we win over the Iraqi people. I didn't quite get it. First, we were to occupy, destroy, kill, then we should reach out for their friendship. I couldn't have imagined a foreign group coming to America with that same agenda. Yet that's what we were being asked to do.

"Win them over," was the strategy. Maybe it worked, or it was possible that I was just the one guy in the class who didn't get it. I just didn't believe the campaign would be effective. We were told to be polite and discreet when dealing with the Iraqi people. As soldiers, it was important not to be seen as acting rude, despite the fact that a high percentage of soldiers had conducted themselves that way in past wars. We were to be diplomats, representing our "Great nation."

Perhaps my understanding was different. What I was hearing was, it didn't matter that our brethren were being killed. We were supposed to go into this war with a positive attitude. This for sure was a new and different army from what I had been used too. I saw it as a quagmire, and not safe. We were told to respect the local people as well as conduct ourselves in an orderly manner at all times. I knew then that would be a difficult challenge for most of the soldiers who were on the plane with me. They were trained to fight. In my own group, some of the most disgusting languages was spoken. The soldiers did not care who was around, or who was listening.

For those reasons, I understood there was a need for a class on conduct and culture. However, I didn't believe one class would do much to change anyone's behavior or mindset of war. In fact, the soldier's only concern, was the war. Cordial language and being a diplomat were pretty much out the window. I finally agreed that it was important to know a few Iraqi phrases. Being able to converse in Arabic, could be a significant survival tactic. In order to perform our duties, it was important to understand a little of what was being said. It would also be useful when monitoring the communications equipment.

Near the end of the week, we were to receive a visit from one of the highest-ranking soldiers in Iraq, General George Casey. He was the commander of the coalition forces in Iraq. But unfortunately, his busy schedule did not allow him to make the trip. Replacing General Casey was one of his deputies, a British major general. He spoke on the subject of molding the Iraqi soldiers. His class included a lot of culturally sensitive issues as well. In short, he was telling us how to work alongside the Iraqi soldiers.

The best was saved for last when there was yet another class on Arabic culture. The instructor was an American enlisted soldier. He was just a couple of pay grades above a private. (Private is lowest pay grade) He wore the rank of a specialist. I will call him Specialist H.

Specialist H. had just received his second master's degree in Arabic studies from the University of Richmond, Virginia. He grew up in Sudan and moved to the United States in his early adult years. While stationed in Iraq, he worked towards his Ph.D. He did not volunteer for duty, in Iraq; he never really wanted to come. However, because of his specialty skills, he was selected to come over. Working as an instructor was not his only duties, he also performed routine duties like any other soldier.

Specialist H. was also a translator for the Central Command in Baghdad. In his few months in the country, he translated at a number of high-level meetings for different commanders. He was quite knowledgeable of the Iraqi people and their way of life. I learned more in four hours from Specialist H. than I did in forty hours from others at Ft McCoy.

Specialist H. could have become an officer and raised his pay grade, however, he said, "I have no desire to be a leader in war." Like many soldiers, including myself, he just wanted to honor his commitment and be done.

The week of mandatory orientation classes at Phoenix Academy was somewhat compelling and informative. A few of the classes were repetitious, but repetition works. It was an eye-opener to see soldiers from different NATO countries working together and running the day-to-day operations. Before my arrival in 2003, there were 150,000 American soldiers in Iraq and another 23,000 from supporting countries. Those numbers decreased by the time I arrived in 2006. The soldiers I saw were mostly from Uganda, Macedonia, and Great Britain. The soldiers from Macedonia were more noticeable, because of their responsibility for guarding the compound.

The staff in charge of training strongly advised us to stay away from the walls and borders protecting the compound. "Getting too close to the walls could be fatal. The Macedonian soldiers had a reputation for being paranoid and trigger happy. Stay away, from the Macedonian soldiers while they are on guard duty. They'd rather shoot first, and ask questions later."

It was rumored that a jogger was shot near the protective barrier of the compound prior to our coming. The guards assumed the jogger was an intruder. They only had to tell me this once. After the warning, I had no intention of going near the walls, or to do any wandering, especially after dark or early morning.

On the last evening of training at the Phoenix Academy, I chose to go to the fitness center. It looked like a safe place to work out, without the fear of being shot. Besides, it was indoors and only a few doors down from the barracks. It was not your most up-to-date fitness center by any means, but it was safer than being outside. The room was small maybe 15 x 20, with two old treadmills, and an old manual stationary bike. There was not much space between the equipment. The room was not bright, having only one dim overhead fluorescent light. Luckily, a large window allowed plenty of sunshine to come through.

A guard tower was just a few meters from the window of the fitness room. The large window faced the guard tower which was on the west side of the compound. Through the window, I was able to see the guard while running on the treadmill. Occasionally, I would catch a glimpse of him looking through the window at me. The story about the trigger-happy guards was fresh on my mind. We were both foreign to each other, and I kept watching him out of the corner of my eye. I avoided making direct eye contact with the guard. A short while later, as I was still running, I was startled by the guard, when he raised his hand to wave at me.

At the same moment when the tower guard waved, the door swung open and two Macedonian soldiers entered the room. My heart was pounding by now. I felt uncomfortable with only the three of us in the room. At that moment, all the horror stories that were told, along with all the unexplained incidents that had happened in Iraq, suddenly flashed through my head. Trying not to reveal my anxiety, I continued to run. But by now I was totally paranoid.

Now I am thinking what if it's a setup? What if the guard in the window radioed for the other two Macedonian soldiers to come down? Instantly, one of the Macedonians in the room gave me a friendly nod. Neither of us could speak the other's language, but the nod he gave was a reassuring gesture. I was relieved.

The other two Macedonians in the room only came to join their colleague. They wanted to work out on the second treadmill, except they had a problem trying to figure out how it operated. I stepped over to give them instructions by simply pushing the buttons. Their smiles expressed their gratitude, and that kind of put me at ease. Although I was feeling more relaxed with the two of them in the room, I continued to watch their every move. I had formed a preconception of the Macedonian soldiers based on the story that was told during the briefing.

I watched with total amazement at how fast the guy was able to run wearing only flip flop shoes. He seemed to be pushing his limits. The flapping sound of his flip flops grew louder each time one of his feet contacted the mat of the treadmill. Along with the flapping sound, each time the belt rotated around the frame of the old semi-rusty treadmill, a sharp piercing squeaky noise was made. It got even louder in the room, as his friend stood by, shouting as if he was encouraging his comrade to go faster.

The door opened again, and this time it was a fellow U.S. soldier who came down to join me. He had a look of surprise on his face when he noticed the Macedonian soldiers running in flip flops. My colleague was an army reservist and a Baptist minister from the western mountains of North Carolina. He made his own attempt to communicate with the Macedonian soldiers. One of them tried to respond by speaking very broken English. This was the same guy who ran in his flip flops on the treadmill. He pointed to my comrade's shoes, smiling and insinuating that he liked them.

At that same moment without reservation, my colleague took off his sneakers and handed them to the Macedonian soldier. The Macedonian soldier hesitated, indicating before accepting the sneakers. He was so thankful that tears ran down his face. I was also touched by my colleague's act of kindness. It truly was one of the kindest acts that I witnessed of a soldier.

I left the fitness room with my comrade to return to the barracks. He walked back on the hot stones with his bare feet. I expressed my admiration for the kind act he did by giving up his shoes. "It's no problem for me, I have another pair, but the poor guy apparently has no way of getting a pair," he told me.

We left the young Macedonian soldier with a bright visual radiating smile on his face. I am sure the Macedonian soldier will never forget the gift from the American soldier.

Before departing the academy, we had one final class. The class was titled "Cultural Sensitivity." The class was taught by the deputy commanding general of the coalition forces in Iraq, who substituted for the commanding general. The class was designed on how to be a successful advisor to the Iraqi army and the specifics of building an Arabic army.

The general emphasized that no one expected us to take an army that has been totally dismantled and rebuilt it. Especially not in comparison to our own army. What was expected, though, was how to build an army just good enough to be called an army. He wanted us to get the job done, and then get out.

The British general said, "You will reach success if you are able to get the Iraqi forces up to fifty percent of your own army." He spoke in terms of skills, and not size. This was the political theory of the entire Coalition Military Training Team (CMATT).

"Only the Iraqis themselves can make improvements over time. The Iraqis will receive plenty of training over the next year. Their success will be determined by their willingness to learn and build their own fighting forces."

The British general's words remained with me throughout the year. His theory was one that I often referred to. I especially referred to his theory whenever one of us got a little stressed when dealing with the Iraqi soldiers. As time passed, I understood the concept of his theory better whenever my team members and I were looking for results from the Iraqis. I met a number of Iraqi soldiers who showed no motivation for fighting or for working together.

9

As soon as the last class ended, we moved out of the Phoenix Academy, making room for the next group of newly arrived soldiers. Everyone said their goodbyes and returned to their assigned teams. Each team departed to different locations throughout Iraq. Sergeant Todd, Colonel Sam, and I were fortunate because we moved less than two kilometers away from the academy, giving us a break from traveling.

The soldiers that we were to replace even drove down to give us a ride. They drove three small white Nissan pickup trucks that were covered with dried mud and dust. The soldiers were excited to give us a ride to our new location. "Pardon the dirty trucks, but there is no need to wash them because of the constant blowing sand and sometimes muddy terrain," one of the sergeants said.

Colonel Sam, Sergeant Todd and I loaded up our bags as the outgoing team members drove us to the Iraqi side of Camp Taji. We were expected to live and work with an estimate of 230 Iraqi soldiers for one year. While helping us set up, the outgoing team explained that as advisors, we were to take charge. We would have contact with three Iraqi interpreters 24/7. That was news to me.

"Oh yes, roll out your sleeping bag and make yourself comfortable for a year," Colonel Sam told me. The conditions on the Iraqi camp were not exactly up to my sanitary standards and needed a lot of work. With its occasional power outages and limited running water in the toilets, I saw the place as a haven for infectious diseases.

One of the sergeants on the outgoing team must have recognized my expression of disappointment. "Hey guys, there are few extra rooms on the coalition side of the camp, and you could probably move there if you like," He was generous enough to drive my battle buddy and myself over to that side of the camp. He showed us the empty rooms and introduced us to a civilian with an Indian accent, who was in charge of the rooms. My battle buddy and I completed the paperwork, signed for the rooms, and received the keys. We rushed back to get our bags to move in. We chose a more environmentally healthy and safer place to live. We were prepared to deal with the consequences for not living on the Iraqi camp, in case any came up.

The area of the camp we moved to was located on the coalition side of Camp Taji. It was nicknamed "Tomahawk Village." Another one of those places renamed by American soldiers. I am not sure how they came up with the name Tomahawk Village. Neither do I know if the name changes remained the same after the American forces left the area. I only know that I came across at least a half dozen nicknames of places during my tour of duty.

The buildings didn't look like the average military barracks. The facilities looked more like an old run-down motel out in a desert village. I wasn't sure how old the building was, nonetheless, they appeared to have been constructed in the early '60s. It was a one-story building with tan bricks that matched the color of the sand. There was a buildup of solid dried mud stuck to the outside walls and around the doors. Each room had one rear window, which was covered with sandbags, to protect us from any small armed munition blast. After seeing the room, I knew immediately lots of cleaning was involved in order to make the place suitable for living.

My team members and I would live next to one another, with the three interpreters living a few doors down in their own rooms. Which explained the twenty-four-hour contact that we would have with the interpreters. They were our voices, 'if you will.' The interpreters were hired and paid by the U.S. government; therefore, they were authorized rooms nearby.

I wanted to unpack, get a shower and start cleaning my room. It had been a while since I was able to lie down in a place of comfort. I was really excited about having a room again, even if it wasn't in the best order. I just wanted to get some much-needed rest.

After a short while of cleaning and unpacking my bags, Sergeant Todd, knocked on the door. He suggested that I come along with him and one of the sergeants from the outgoing team. They ask me to go out for tea and meet the Iraqis. They wanted to go over to the Iraqi school, where we would be working for the next year. It was already around 20:30, and as usual, if the opportunity was there to get rest, I always choose rest over any night time activity. It had been so long since I'd been alone, and I just wanted to enjoy the comfort. I declined the invitation. They probably thought I was being rude, but no, I was being me. I needed my time and suggested that we all meet for breakfast the following morning.

It was on the 1st of July, 2006 when we had our official introduction to the members of the outgoing team. We met just outside the rooms. We gathered around a wooden table that they had built from scrap lumber they found on the Iraqi camp. After the introductions, we all left for breakfast. It was obvious from the smiles on their faces, that they were happy. Now that we had arrived, they only had a few days left in Iraq.

I guess there was some progress made towards meeting the mission's requirements. There were seven members on the outgoing team, and only three of us were sent to replace them. They were eager to show off the Iraqi soldiers and what they had accomplished during the last year. Right after breakfast, we drove directly to the location of the Iraqi school where the outgoing team had been working. Nervous was an understatement for describing the way I felt prior to meeting the Iraqi soldiers. I had heard many rumors about the Iraqi people. The speculation that the Iraqi army was infiltrated with terrorist, was the most bothersome. That one report alone was enough to get my anxiety juices flowing.

Never mind all the culture classes, I was not sure how to conduct myself during the first meeting. My intentions were to give a good first impression and to be a good representative for my country. My feelings of being nervous lasted only for a few moments. It was after seeing how my fellow service members interacted with the Iraqi soldiers. Only then was I able to recompose. They joked around with each other, giving high-fives, and slapping one another on their backsides.

The most interesting group of Iraqis I met on my first day on the camp, were the three interpreters. Since they were already in place, there was no need for them to move. They were all of Iraqi descent, and as I would later find out, two of the three had lived outside Iraq. Hani spent a few years in Syria and Omar was educated and spent a number of years in Great Britain. Omar still possessed a British passport. The three of them were young, and their style of dress, baseball caps, western jeans, and even some of the terminology they used, led me to believe that they had adopted many forms of western life.

We were officially introduced by the outgoing sergeant major. He drove Sergeant Todd and myself to the Iraqi Noncommissioned Officers (NCOs) quarters. Their quarters consisted of only three rooms with eight soldiers per room. The sergeant major introduced us to each Iraqi NCO. The first thing the Iraqi NCOs did was to offer tea. The offering of tea to their guest is a tradition of the Iraqi people. We sat at a folding card table in the crowded room. Obviously, not all the Iraqi NCOs were able to fit into the small hot room. Only the top-ranking Iraqi NCOs were the ones who got to have a seat at the table.

We went around the room as everyone introduced themselves, and expressed how happy they were to have the opportunity to be working together for the next year. I didn't say I was happy to be there, I only said "nice to meet you." I wasn't being a jerk, it was just too premature for me to say I was happy.

The site that the school was located on was not large at all. I estimated it to be half the size of a soccer field. The former team members had unofficially named the school the "Alamo," taken from the Alamo in San Antonio Texas. It was designed in a rectangular shape with limited classroom space, and only two administrative offices. The good news was that the coalition forces hired contractors to renovate another site to take the place of that site, adding more space.

Many other facilities were being renovated all across Iraq mostly by NATO hired contractors. The newly renovated facilities were part of an agreement between the coalition and the Iraqi government.

During the tour of the school, I was shown the office where I was to work, along with Colonel Sam, and Sergeant Todd. It was a small room with five desks. Two were lined up on one wall, and the three others faced two large windows, covered by blinds having at least an inch of dust on them. There were five computers, one refrigerator, and a noisy clanging ceiling fan, that was poorly mounted to the ceiling and shook as if it would fall down at any moment.

The toilets were located just next door from the office area. The unpleasant smell was the lone giveaway to its location. They were squat toilets. You squatted instead of sitting comfortably on a bowl. A custom that I never adapted to. There was only a tile pan with an opening on the same level as the floor. With little or no water for it to function was the main cause of the unpleasant odor.

Over a period of time, I accepted the unsuitable conditions of the building. I was thankful for the refrigerator and the noisy fan. The refrigerator kept the bottles of water cool, providing there was electricity. The fan was important for survival since the air conditioning system was not working. But it was the noises that came from the fan, that I came to appreciate. The noise kept me awake, more than fan did in keeping me cool.

The outgoing team members continued to work out of the room until their departure, making it even more crowded. I was to replace a young captain, who was being reassigned back to his unit located in Germany. He was on temporary duty in Iraq. Because personnel allotments had decreased, I was to take over his duties, overseeing personnel and logistics. That entailed keeping the books and paying the Iraqi translators. It was important that I kept a complete record of their time sheets and an accurate record of their schedule. This was to ensure that they continued to receive their monthly salary in an honest and timely manner.

Rami was the third translator and as soon as he discovered that I was assigned to keep their accounts, he wanted to get better acquainted with me. It was his way of ensuring that I would do the right thing when it came to his money. Rami was close to five feet tall, with dark brown eyes and short kinky hair. He had a little round belly, that showed that he did not skip any of his American meals. The meals were one of benefits that he received while working as a translator. Another major benefit was free medical care, from the U.S. facility on the camp.

"Nice to meet you, sergeant. Do you plan to make any changes to our work schedules, or our pay?" Rami was straightforward. I was somewhat surprised by his boldness. He was establishing himself as the leader of the group.

"It is much too early for me to answer your questions," I told him. "Please allow me time to review the system as it is."

I discussed my concerns with the outgoing captain and assured him that I would probably continue things his way unless Colonel Sam required me to make changes.

A few hours later we had our first official meeting with more Iraqi soldiers. The temperature outside was sizzling. We all gathered in the headquarters section of the Iraqi school, which were just steps outside the door of my office and that foul-smelling toilet. Because this was my first business meeting, I was nervous because I didn't know what to expect.

I wondered why would the army entrust me with so much responsibility. They replaced an active-duty army captain and a sergeant major, with two reserved sergeants. I felt that I was about to take on more responsibilities than I could handle. However, both the captain and the sergeant major assured us that given a little time, our team would do well.

I had just met these guys, and I was not sure why they would say that I would do well. They knew nothing about me. I think that they were just anxious to leave Iraq. It probably did not matter to them who took over their responsibilities. I totally understood and I did not fault them for wanting to leave that place.

Before they could leave, they had to get my team members and myself up to a point where we were able to take over. The captain introduced me to the Iraqi soldiers and explained through a translator that I would be replacing him. He requested that the Iraqi soldiers start dealing with me from that moment on. He mentioned to them that he would still be around for a couple more days. He felt it was the best way for everyone to get familiar with one another.

Things were moving fast, and I had just assumed a major task, with no way out. I didn't expect to play such a responsible role in an operation that would later have a large impact on the training of the Iraqi soldiers.

10

A soldier should always be ready to answer the call for duty. I spent many years preparing to do just that. One main objective of the military is to ensure that soldiers are prepared both mentally and physically to answer the call of duty.

I will argue that training differentiates from reality. When your day of training is done, you're done and you were dismissed. However, real-world combat is not like training. In real-world combat, no one knows when their day might end, or how it might end. The training I received was important, but it did not prepare me for the challenges I had to face in Iraq.

The basics of the training and how to survive in warfare were helpful, but I also relied on my life skills to help me deal with some of the challenges. In particular my communication skills. Those skills came in pretty handy when dealing with the Iraqi soldiers. I had a degree in Justice Policy Studies. There were some similarities, but my people skills and a second career in law enforcement was more helpful. I got lots of practice back home on the job when encountering people who had run-ins with the law.

However, in Iraq, everything was forever evolving. I am sure I wasn't the only one who had difficulties adapting to the changes. It was apparent that everyone handled their emotions differently. Many soldiers in the unit were already beyond midlife. It seemed that we all had different attitudes about being deployed. I no longer possessed that "be all you can be," or that rock solid soldier mentally that soldiers usually have. That was the mentality of many young soldiers who were just starting out in their military career. The majority of guys in the unit were more than halfway through their career. We were known as "citizen soldiers, or weekend warriors." We were expected to balance our lives between being a civilian and being a soldier.

Being a soldier, meant that life was forever evolving. The gunfight that I experienced on my first day in Iraq, were reasons for my mind and body being on high alert, twenty-four hours a day. From that day forward, I was constantly adapting to all the changes.

Being briefed on my duties and told what was expected of me, heightened my tensions even more. Especially after discovering that I would live and work with the Iraqi soldiers every day. At the time, I was not prepared to do that. My partnership with the interpreters was a cultural awakening in itself. Our time together would likely extend beyond the normal eight hours that most workers spend together. In order to accomplish what was expected, we had to have access to each other, twenty-four hours a day. Not only would I have to rely on the interpreters to translate, but there may be times that I would have to rely on the interpreters in finding solutions to problems that I may encounter.

Days passed, and the outgoing team finally left Iraq. They were missed by the team and the interpreters just days after their departure. I had to get used to working alone without the assistance of the captain. I was there to assist and advise the Iraqi soldiers. The captain was right, I had to seek the advice of the interpreters early on while dealing with the Iraqi soldiers. Their advice may not have been the best, but it was useful. It was just one of the reasons for building a profound trust with the interpreters. We spent many days and nights pondering some difficult situations.

Breakfast with the interpreters and my team members became a daily protocol. We'd gather to discuss the business of the day without the Iraqi soldiers present. The meetings at the breakfast table were one of two enjoyable moments of the day. For one thing, my mind was clearer in the morning and I was able to prepare for all the hustle and bustle of the day.

Another favorite time of my day was meeting with the Iraqi soldiers for chai during break and after work. It seemed that's when they were more open to sharing stories about their lives, their families, as well as discussing politics. What they considered as priorities, did not differ from any other member of the human race: their God, family, income, and vacation. The Iraqis truly loved their families. Their love extended beyond their intimate family and included all family members as well. Rami told me that the alliances among their ethnic groups were just as strong.

Their strong bonds with their family were likely key to their motivation to survive. Both Rami and Hani were surprised when the Iraqi soldiers shared stories about their personal life with me.

"Sergeant Slade, I have to tell you that it is not normal for an Iraqi to discuss their private life with anyone who is not a family member. They think you are a nice guy, so they tell you. Some of them even believe that you are Iraqi, in the American army." Hani burst out laughing after he finished his statement.

I am not sure of the reason why, but on more than one occasion, a small group of the Iraqi soldiers who were assigned to the camp would tell me personal stories about their lives. You know Hani, I said, maybe they share stories because of their desperation, and hopeless situations. It's likely that they just need someone other than another Iraqi soldier to talk to.

Even in the short time that Rami and Hani knew me, I made them aware of the numerous times they would bring up the idea of leaving for Syria. I told them, that the soldiers were no different. Like you, and Rami, maybe they want to get away as well. They are probably fed up with all the chaos and they are likely seeking relief from the conflict. Hani, you need to understand that the war has affected everyone.

My most intense discussions with the Iraqi soldiers took place during chai breaks. During that time many of the Iraqi soldiers were relaxed and more open to talking about some of their most private concerns. One topic a few of them talked about that raised my eyebrows, was moving to Iran. They felt that conditions in Iran had to be better than those in their own country. "There are no bombs being dropped in Iran, not many people are being killed, and it's safe to go to the market." One of the Iraqi soldiers said in broken English.

Sergeant Mohammed was lying on his neatly made bunk. The back of his head was sunk deep into his pillow and his arms folded across his chest. He shook his head from left to right as a sign of his disapproval. "I don't like Iran," he mumbled. He was critical of Iran for its war with Iraq, back in the eighties.

I understand, guys, but there is not much I can do but listen, I said. Speaking through Hani's interpretation, I let both the Iraqi soldiers and the interpreters know that I could understand what they were feeling. Nevertheless, I was not in their shoes. My situation was different. I am here with you, I see your struggles, and I pray along with you for peace. It was a meaningful moment we shared, and I thought it was important to let them know how I felt. It was another way of earning their trust.

I watched the Iraqi soldiers who showed up for radio communications training each day. Many looked mentally exhausted from the endeavors of war and life. They operated under dire conditions while trying to survive, and having many odds against them. Underneath their weary looking faces, they still managed to find something to smile about, despite their lives being interrupted by the devastation of war.

Their country was in ruins. Their infrastructure had been demolished. For those reasons, they struggled, while trying to provide for themselves and their families. On top of those issues, they had to disguise themselves from the general population of Iraqis, to avoid being seen as collaborating with the Americans. I gave them credit for their endurance while trying to withstand the deteriorating conditions that they were engulfed by.

The Iraqi soldiers were very in-tune to their surroundings, which in some ways led them to be suspicious of each other. I didn't quite understand how they could work and train together, or even stand among the same ranks under those conditions. Their actions led me to have my own concerns about trusting them or the interpreters on occasion. Never mind my feelings, I along with my team members had to rely on both the soldiers and the interpreters alike in order to get things done.

In the same manner, the Iraqi soldier's doubtfulness of each other did not take away from their combine intellectual skills to accomplish their training task. Many knew a lot more than I did about the communication equipment, as well as their mission, which was providing battlefield communications to their field commanders. Several Iraqi soldiers spoke more than one language. That was more than my team members or I could do. I regret the fact that I was not able to communicate directly with them. I think we would have been more conscious of each other's true feelings.

"Salaam" one Iraqi soldier muttered as we passed each other on the walkway. He bowed his head and tapped his chest, with his hand positioned over his heart. He was saluting me, with a peaceful smile on his face. I could tell the salute was genuine.

Encounters like those led me to believe that not all Iraqis were Islamic radicals; filled with hatred, as some who wore the same uniform as I did, would like to have had me to believe. The world the Iraqis were forced to live in, was full of violence and suffering.

Nearly all Iraqi soldiers encountered some form of violence daily. Not all of what they experienced happened on the battlefield. As a result of extreme radicals infiltrating the Iraqi Army, they were not safe on the camp either. A majority lived in unsafe neighborhoods. When they traveled back home, I was told that they had to sneak in and out of their houses. They put themselves in danger just by showing up on the camp.

After the rotation the Iraqi soldiers or one of the interpreters, would gather and talk about their adventures. At the end of one particular duty day, I was invited to stop by the Iraqi barracks for chai. We were having a conversation about the violence in Baghdad, when suddenly, Sergeant Mohammed jumped up onto his bare feet, wearing only a brown army tee shirt and the trousers of his battle dress uniform. He made direct eye contact with me and shouted while waving the palm of his hand. "Sergeant Slade! I swear to Allah, that there are so many people killed in Baghdad every day; many, many, I swear to Allah! And you want to know what happens? Nothing Sergeant Slade!" Sergeant Mohamed showed so much emotion when he spoke. I was both shocked, and surprised, as I listened to him.

"I am not upset with you," he said, looking at the expression on my face. "I am upset with the American and the Iraqis *damn-* system!" He said in very broken English.

"Yeah, people just killing people," Rami added.

After hearing about their misery, I felt guilty complaining about my own sorrows of life and being in Iraq. In contrast to the hardships that the Iraqis endured, I was better off. They lived a much different life than me. I was blessed to be living in a peaceful nation with my family.

Knowing I had a peaceful home to return to, was my main drive to survive. But, the Iraqi soldiers and the interpreters did not have that assurance. There was never any certainty about what they might find when they traveled back to their neighborhoods.

Colonel Tee, who was the Iraqi Commandant of the training school, was no different from the others. When he would return from a trip to Baghdad, he too would find the time to update me on some of his own adventures, that took place.

93

I knew nothing about where Hani's neighborhood was, but I assumed it wasn't located in a safe section of the city. Every two weeks one of the interpreters would rotate with the group of Iraqi soldiers. Once after Hani's rotation when he returned to the camp, I ask him about his trip to the city. He tilted his head back and looked up to the heavens. He tapped his heart with his right hand, and without hesitation, he answered, "Two or three missing this time." I didn't have to ask him what he meant by two or three missing. I knew he was referring to the death of someone close.

Hani stepped closer, I could see that he was still shaken from his trip home. He said, "Sergeant Slade, me and my family barricaded ourselves into our home. My family will be staying with my uncle for a few days," he whispered. He did not want the others to hear what he was saying, because he did not want to share his grief with the Iraqi soldiers, besides he didn't trust them.

After a period, anything that he told was no surprise, because he had already informed me that some of his neighbors were supporters of the militants. He was afraid that they would eventually find out about what he did for a living.

Sometimes the soldiers returned to the camp describing the gun fights that took place right in front of their residences. Others would recall the numerous bodies they saw lying on the street. For those reasons, it never surprised me, when one of the Iraqi soldiers or an interpreter reported back to the camp, hours, or even days late for duty.

"Under Saddam Hussein's rule, those things would not have happened," Rami said.

"The children are not safe walking to school alone. There were not nearly as many bombings carried out in the city, or in the whole country for that matter. Saddam kept the people of Iraq under control. I could even walk my girl through the park at night, without any fear," boasted Rami.

We seemed to have had more discussion of negative incidents, than those of positive ones. There were just not too many positive things happening at the time. I thought the group discussions were good for us all, even more during the difficult times. Both the Iraqi and the coalition sides of the camps became increasingly dangerous, due to the escalation of attacks on the ground. The insurgents got braver, and it did not matter whether it was day or night when they launched their assaults.

There were nights when I jumped into bed, seeking refuge from the sounds of mortars, and other massive explosions. I would lay in bed listening to the friendly forces set up their heavy equipment just hundreds of meters away from my window. Once they set up they returned direct fire towards the enemy. I could hear the sounds of the big cannons and mortar shells as they were launched well after midnight.

I tossed and turned from side-to-side in my bunk. I covered my head with my pillow, hoping to drown out the sounds of the artillery cannons. It seemed as if nothing was able to reduce the pounding rumbling of the artillery shells. I laid still, fixed in one position, waiting for the noise to end. I laid there until the wee hours of the morning before it all finally stopped.

Camp Taji was a major army aviation airfield located only 28 kilometers from Baghdad. It's location and some of the sensitive missions that originated from there made it a main target for the militants. It was apparent that the favorite targets of the enemy were pipelines, airfields, and housing units. These were the places that they were likely to do the most damage. Both sides of the camp, the Iraqi and the coalition side, was always on alert.

There was one episode when I could hear rockets randomly raining down into the massive junkyard, meters away from my building. When missiles would hit, the ear-splitting blast they made were thunderous and alarming. The whole building shook. At times I wanted to jump out of bed and run outside to escape. My thoughts were short-lived. I came to my senses and realized I would be safer inside.

When I was able to walk outside, the sun was rapidly rising up from the horizon, and everything seemed very strange. It was quiet, all the activities had stopped. I could smell the burning of rubber. No one was around, and the heavy artillery equipment had disappeared. It was peaceful, if not for the rising thick black smoke over the junkyard, it appeared as if nothing had happened. At one point I thought I was awakening from a dream. But, my ears were ringing as proof that it was not a dream.

Those were atrocious nights. But a few soldiers claimed to have slept right through it all. The fighters went back into hiding, only to regroup and wait until the next night to start all over. There were always reasons to be on alert, anticipating a mortar or a missile attack. Life was unpredictable in that part of the world.

During those times, I kept telling myself to hold on, 'conditions are harsh, but I got to hold on.' I prayed an awful lot, because I felt alone, and trapped in a place that I did not want to be.

With so much happening I had to mentally clock out from all the disorder. I needed a break to evaluate myself and my surroundings. My trust in the Iraqi soldiers diminished a bit. I had vivid thoughts of insurgents hiding in the ranks of the Iraqi Army. My thoughts could have been irrational, but something told me to withdraw for a period. I didn't share my feelings with other soldiers, for fear of being seen as paranoid. Soldiers are supposed to be seen as warriors and having thick skin. Because of the intensity of my emotions on occasion, I didn't always fit that description. Slowing down helped me to re-energize, both mentally and physically.

My trips to the Iraqi side of the camp were less frequent. I worked from the coalition side of the camp as much as possible for some days. I waited for the rocket attacks to cool down before resuming my duties at the training school.

Once again, I became skeptical of the interpreters. I was not sure if they were the ones informing the militants of the locations of their targets. I stopped sharing information about myself, or the work schedule with them. I reminded myself not to get too close. I just thought it was best to step back. They probably were trustworthy, after all, they had been cleared by the US State Department. Despite the fact that I was required to work with interpreters around the clock every day, at times I felt I was getting too close. It's likely that I was a little paranoid, but my reasoning for not sharing certain information, 'it was better to be safe than sorry.'

After a while when things cooled down, I had to catch up on my additional duties. Those duties involved making occasional trips to the Green Zone, located in Baghdad. I was reluctant to leave Camp Taji. The camp had become my place of comfort. I had to report to headquarters to pick up cash in U.S. currency, in order to purchase supplies for the Iraqi school. The first thing I had to do was to plan the trip.

The traveling to the capital was the most difficult part of the trip. It was impossible to walk out the door and jump in a vehicle. Days before I needed to leave, I went to the flight terminal and signed up for a flight in advance. Even on that occasion, a seat wasn't always guaranteed. Other soldiers and contractors were always flying throughout the country for various reasons. I could have easily traveled in one of the tactical vehicles that went out on daily patrols. However, given the choice between a tactical vehicle or a helicopter flight, I chose the helicopter flight. I saw it as being a safe and quicker mode of transportation.

The daily intelligence reports, confirmed my suspicions of the dangers that I might have encountered while riding in a ground vehicle. It was reported that there were suspicions of numerous improvised explosive devices (IED's) placed alongside the roadway. On that account, I made the right decision to fly. I always had my doubts about riding in a vehicle, knowing that any moment a booby trap could explode.

When the time came for my flight, I gladly drove the half kilometer and reported to the air hanger. Moments after my arrival, my name was called. I was all decked out in my battle rattle gear. Everything I was not wearing, was packed inside my duffle bag. It was a requirement for soldiers to travel with the essential combat gear, in the event that they or the camp, came under attack. I dragged my heavy duffle bag across the unpaved grounds of the airfield. I was rushed to board an already highly accelerated helicopter with its rotors rapidly spinning and blowing sand in every direction.

I was barely able to toss my heavy duffle bag onto the helicopter before it lifted off. I climbed on board while pulling up my body, as I slid along the floor. I was drenched in sweat. One of the gunners saw me struggling and gave me a hand getting into my seat. He then assisted me with strapping myself in. Thank you, I said, even though I knew he could not hear me because of the loud roaring of the engine. I am not sure if I would have made it without his assistance.

The chopper was crowded with one other passenger and his baggage. This was my first time flying in a helicopter gunship, especially over a live battlefield. Therefore, I had no idea what to expect. The other helicopters that I had flown in were cargo ships. This one was much smaller and built for attack purposes, and wasn't built to carry more than three or four passengers. There were two gunners in the ready positions on the left and right side of the helicopter. Their job was to protect the chopper from the enemy fire below.

The sun had just set, and it got dark fast. It was difficult to see anything down on the ground, with the exception of a few sparkling lights below. The gunners wore night vision goggles, enabling them to have a better vision of any ground activity.

Glancing out of the door on my right, I could see the red blinking light of a twin helicopter that we were being escorted by. The whole country of Iraq was classified as a combat zone. It was required whenever a helicopter flew in a combat zone, that an escort flew along with it. It was a defensive tactic in the event one of the other came under attack, which happened often in Iraq. The possibility that the helicopter could have been fired on, stayed on my mind during the entire flight.

The roar of the engine grew louder and the seats felt harder. I felt most uncomfortable as the pilot guided the helicopter on a direct path to the Green Zone. In the end, the flight turned out not to be that long. We were only in the air for about 20 to 25 minutes. However, during that short time, the flight was one of the most intoxicating thrills I have ever experienced.

As we got closer to Baghdad, the lights on the ground grew brighter. Looking down, I saw reflections coming off the Tigris River. The bright full moon had a dazzling effect on the water, causing it to sparkle like tiny diamonds floating on its top. We flew directly over it for a short period of time.

The city of Baghdad was much larger than what I expected it to be. As we got closer to the capital, the illumination of lights made it possible for me to distinguish the structures more clearly. Lots of the residential buildings had bright fluorescent bulbs mounted on the side of their exterior walls, similar to some commercial buildings, I was accustomed to seeing in large cities in the U.S.

As the helicopter descended closer to the ground, I noticed that in one area of the city that nearly every building had a mid-size satellite dishes on its rooftop. I counted as many as five dishes on one single roof. Once Rami alluded to the fact that under Saddam's regime satellite dishes were restricted from use for two reasons. The first reason; all communications were controlled by the government. The second reason; they were not attractive. I agreed with the second reason.

99

Looking out of the right door of the helicopter, I could see that we were rapidly approaching the infamous Green zone. The Green zone was located right in the middle of the capital and was encircled by walls of tall concrete pillars, transforming it to a heavily fortified fortress. Before the NATO forces occupied the buildings, a few of them were already surrounded by some type of barriers, which were in place to protect Saddam Hussein and his advisory council from those who wanted to do harm.

I was relieved that my short flying adventure was coming to an end and that the Green zone was the first stop. More importantly, I was glad I arrived without incident. The helicopter approached the airfield, without coming to a complete stop, it hovered a few feet above the ground. I moved to the door, tossing my heavy bags off, and took a small leap onto the ground, keeping my head down for fear of connecting with the swirling rotors.

Once on the ground, the other passenger grabbed his bags and walked in a different direction. Dragging my duffle bag, I walked into a makeshift terminal where I was given instructions. I checked my bags and was assigned a bunk out back in a large tent.

I was a little disappointed, as a guest I thought I might get a nice room with a cozy bed, but it did not happen. A foreign nationalist, who worked as a hotel guardian took great pleasure in giving me directions to a dusty tent out back. He wore a wide smile and spoke with a broken authoritative English accent.

"Sir," he called out. "You will find the toilet and the shower facilities located in the white trailers a few meters behind the tent." The gentleman stood proudly, appearing to be in love with his job, and to let me know that the Green Zone was all business. His actions alone were an indirect way of letting me know that my pay-grade, nor did my stature warrant me a bed elsewhere. I found my way to the tent and discovered that there were a number of soldiers who were also temporarily sleeping in tents.

Spending a night in the tent was a reminder that being in the Green Zone wasn't a break or time off. I was there to conduct business, and the treatment from the hotel guardian brought me back to that reality. He made me aware that I was still in a dangerous environment. It was more dangerous than Camp Taji. The Green Zone was constantly on the alert for incoming rockets and mortar attacks. It was rumored that weeks before my arrival a couple of lives were lost from direct hits.

I was up at dawn the next day and noticed that people were already on the move. They were moving in all directions. Most were soldiers like me, decked out in their battle rattle gear rushing to duty, or to attend to other matters. As I made my way from one side of the compound to the other, I managed to take time out to take a few photos, and check out the sights. The Green zone was incomparable to Camp Liberty, and the other camps. It was the headquarters for the Multinational Security Transition Command in Iraq. They did strategic planning for all operations in Iraq, and security was extremely tight.

The palace grounds were enormous with grass in some places. The patchy spots of grass were outnumbered by bare spots of sandy soil that extended across the lawn. The landscape was made up of man-made waterfronts, and fountains surrounded by a few dried-up palm trees. The trees had been scorched from the blazing sun. Given the environment, the lawn was rather appealing.

The main attraction was the large palace that stood in the center of it all. It displayed obvious remnants of the war. However, looking beyond all the damage, I could see the stunning beauty that it once exhibited. This time there was no problems entering the main building. The NATO forces had taken up occupancy in the building, converting it into a major military operations center for the command. I entered the palace through a triple set of giant mahogany sculptured doors. My eyes were wide open to the amazement of what I saw. The walls and floors were crafted with a mixture of wood panels and

101

patterned white masonry marble. In the middle of the ceiling hung a giant crystal chandelier, with three smaller matching chandeliers encircling it.

The further I wandered into the palace, the more awed I became. Large Persian rugs were mounted on the towering walls and laid out on the floors adding to the beauty. When I walked into the toilet, I continued to be mesmerized by what I was seeing. The mirrors and the toilet seats were trimmed in gold. In fact, all of the toilet fixtures were solid gold. Mounted on the walls were small crystal chandeliers, giving off reflections of rainbows in the mirrors. I am not sure what the other American soldiers felt after seeing the palace, but for a guy like me coming from a small town in North Carolina, I was in disbelief.

11

It was the first day of August in 2006, and the Iraqi soldiers at the training school were excited that the day had finally arrived. It was the day of the grand opening. For many, it was long overdue. Lots of physical, mental and political work was involved in getting the school ready. Colonel Tee had already decorated the school while anticipating the guest to come down for an open house and the celebration.

The moment Sergeant Todd and I walked inside the renovated school with Colonel Tee for a pre-inspection, and my attitude changed. Colonel Tee was pleased, and Sergeant Todd was not so sure, and withheld his comments "This place is better than the Alamo," Colonel Tee said trying to convince us that he was satisfied. Not all the work was completed, but according to the contractor's, the training school was ready to be moved in.

The smell of fresh paint was still lingering through the halls of the building. The exterior walls were painted a bright enamel white, and trimmed in a light enamel baby blue. Inside, the rectangular hallways were painted a bright sunny enamel yellow, and the window frames were bright baby blue. Neither of those would have been my choice of colors, but I had to agree with the colonel, it was better than the old place.

Perhaps I was the only one who noticed the deficiencies since I was the only one to comment on them. I was just being honest about the things that still needed improvement. I thought the amateur American and British contractors did a poor job of painting and cleaning things up. The painters made a mess, by leaving droplets along the edges of the floor, and the trim work was not perfect. They ended up putting a band-aid on an old broken building.

"Sergeant Slade, could you cool it with the comments? We should be focusing on the importance of the events today," Colonel Sam said while holding back his comments.

"Sir, I am only pointing out the poor work done by the contractors. They came here to make a fast buck off the government, and it looks like they succeeded." I muttered, underneath my breath. I wanted Colonel Sam to hear; what I had to say next, so I spoke louder. "The Iraqi soldiers with no experience could have done a better job."

The Colonel wanted to hear none of it. With a frown on his face, he said, "Sergeant Slade, please don't spoil the ceremony with any of your opinions, this is the bread and butter of the mission. Besides, there will be some important people here today."

I simply smirked back, using that expression when I wanted to stir things up. I understand sir, but if I do get out of hand, what are they going to do, send me to Iraq? I asked.

"Come on now, sergeant," Colonel Sam said, laughing out loud.

The ceremony took place in a detached classroom on the northern end of the school grounds. As a result, many of the attendees, weren't able to see the shortcomings that I saw earlier. As always, the Iraq commandant, Colonel Tee, attempted to spiff things up whenever he knew that company was coming.

The doorway of the conference room had a yellow ribbon tied across its entrance. The food was plentiful, and the tables were set up elegantly, with bright white table cloths. Silk flowers were on the designated tables where the generals would sit.

"Sergeant Slade, how do the flowers look?" Colonel Tee asked me.

They look nice, placed between the large dishes of food, I said.

Colonel Tee ordered the food from the best dining facility on the Iraqi Camp. The aroma from the warm food filled the room. The fresh fruit, and the dates that were hand-picked from a tree right outside the building, were overflowing in the baskets on each table.

"Why are you working so hard Colonel Tee, and why so much food?" Omar asked as he took notice. "The officers won't even take time to eat, and besides they're only coming here to be noticed themselves," Omar added, sounding a little jealous. He did not want Colonel Tee to succeed or receive credit for anything. I wasn't sure if their dislike for one another was a cultural problem or not. But Colonel Tee and Omar let it be known, that there was no love between the two of them.

Omar was at odds with Colonel Tee. He believed that the colonel was one of the officers who infiltrated the ranks of the Iraqi Army. For those reasons, Omar never really trusted any of the Iraqi officers. Now Omar; Colonel Sam requested that everyone be on their best behavior during the ceremony, and that includes you, I reminded him.

Colonel Tee was aware of Omar's bitter feelings towards him. However, he was not about to let anything or anyone get in the way of the opening ceremony. He was all decked out as he waited for the ceremony to begin. Colonel Tee stood there looking very sharp and his chest was aligned with medals that he had been awarded for his significant accomplishments throughout his military career. He even trimmed and waxed his thick black mustache.

All the distinguished guests stood around waiting as well, waiting for the ribbon cutting to take place. The highest-ranking official present from the Iraqi Army had the honors. It happened to be one of the Iraqi Generals from the Green Zone. I had no idea who he was, and neither did the interpreters.

However, he had to be important, because all the Iraqi soldiers who were present were very excited.

The opening of the training school was a great accomplishment for the Iraqi Government, the Iraqi Army, the US Government, and both the former team as well as my team. Despite my critiques and comments, I too wanted nothing less than success for the Iraqi soldiers.

Some very high-ranking Iraqi officers showed up for the ceremony. They stood there looking like showmen. Their uniforms were clean; they had fresh haircuts and their faces were closely shaved. That wasn't the norm for them. They usually walked around with muddy boots and worn out BDUs. They greeted one another while hoping for an opportunity for a photo with one of the generals. I agreed with Omar, there were a few who were only there to seek approval. It was the first time that I had seen so many Iraqi Officers in one place. It was also the first time that some of them showed up on Camp Taji for anything.

No one expected the insurgents to halt their activities because of the ceremony. For that reason, security on the Camp was tight. Everything was in order except for one crucial resource, which was electricity. There was not enough fuel on the camp to provide generator power to the other buildings. Due to an increase in attacks, sabotage, and the crippling damage to the infrastructure near the camp, the fuel trucks were not able to get fuel to the generators.

As a result, Colonel Tee ordered that only the generator for the main building be used during the ceremony. The Iraqi soldiers had gotten used to being without power. A few weeks before the ceremony the school had started operating only for a couple of hours each day. Colonel Tee was not discouraged and he always found a way to stay positive. He certainly did not let the fuel issues affect the opening ceremony.

From the commanding general down to the lowest ranking soldier, everyone was excited over moving into the larger training facility. From the looks on the Iraqi soldiers' faces and decorations throughout the building, one would not know that a war was going on outside. Upon completion of the ribbon cutting and a few speeches by the Iraqi Generals, time was taken out to celebrate the occasion. In spite of their mutual dislike of each other, the Iraqi officers seemed to have enjoyed themselves. At least that was the impression I got watching the different ethnic groups. Never mind that I had been working with the Iraqi soldiers for a few months already, it wasn't easy to detect the division among them in the room.

I remember Omar leaning across the table to tell Sergeant Todd and I, that "The ceremony will do nothing to bring these divided groups together, and nothing will change. They just don't like each other."

I felt the distrust among the Iraqi soldiers up close. Almost all of them came from different ethnic groups and far away cities from across the country. The two main religious groups, the Sunni and Shiites refused to sit at the same table. Colonel Tee was aware of that in his planning. He had already prepared separate tables on different sides of the room.

The festivities were winding down, and soon it was time to get back to work. There was a great deal of business that needed attending to before the duty day was over. However, I did not feel comfortable moving on without mentioning the shoddy work that was done by the contractors once more. It was something that needed addressing among the commanders, especially the American commanders. Our mission was to prepare the Iraqi soldiers to stand alone and fight their fight. There were a lot of US dollars invested in renovating the training school and from what I saw, that was a mistake.

"Colonel Sam, I'd like you to be honest with me, and tell me what you think about the work that went into renovating the building?" I asked

"I think it looks okay," was all he said.

That's my point, Colonel Sam, the workers, only tried to make things look okay. But the structural and the electrical work looked to be hazardous, and shabby. Back home I had seen a few old houses, and buildings renovated over the years, and I knew what I was seeing there was not safe.

"We are here to support the Iraqis and see that they are in a position to run their military, and nothing more, and for me, that's good enough," Colonel Sam said.

I was surprised that Colonel Sam didn't demand more of the contractors. However, on the other hand, this wasn't his first deployment, and working with defense contractors. He probably had some idea of their traditional work habits. But he was in a position to demand better work, because he was the only and the highest-ranking, U.S. commanding officer at the training school.

"Colonel Sam, you have the power to get things corrected, and not let the contractors get away with ripping off the American taxpayers," I said.

There was an abundance of work that needed to be completed, such as concrete repair, doors, and a few windows needed replacing. Also, the painting was incomplete and needed finishing before the contractors could claim their mission was complete. Nevertheless, the Iraqi soldiers and Colonel Tee were happy with what they got. I guess they accepted the fact that anything was better than the war-torn structure that they were used too. For the Iraqi soldiers, the renovated building was ideal for their living and working conditions, and it seemed to be enough to satisfy Colonel Sam.

The contractors got paid and moved on, leaving behind many unresolved maintenance issues. On occasion, before they left, I spoke with them and they were like many other contract workers at the camp. They wanted to complete the job, get paid, and get out of harm's way. I was sure that they knew that back in the US and Britain, that their work would have been unacceptable.

Moving into the school was only one step. There was much more work to be done before our mission was anywhere near complete. Getting more soldiers enrolled in school was important. That entailed keeping the school a safe place for the Iraqi soldiers to live and to train.

Omar did not think enrollment would continue to be high as long as Colonel Tee was the commandant. He was not pleased with the praise that Colonel Tee had received from the Iraqi general, for his contributions to the training school. "Not many soldiers want to risk their lives traveling through the country to come down to this corrupted school," Omar said, smiling like an envious kid. "So now that you have this new building what are your plans for getting more soldiers to come here?" Omar turned to Colonel Tee and asked in English, to ensure that Sergeant Todd and I were listening.

"Omar, that is not your worry! Your job is to translate and not to run the school. I would like it best if you would stay out of my business!" Colonel Tee shouted back in English and a few words in Arabic.

I stayed out of their fight. However, I knew Colonel Tee worked hard trying to make sure that everything was in order. Colonel Tee spent many hours in the Green Zone trying to convince both American and Iraqi commanders to increase spending for the training school. He needed more supplies for the school.

However, Omar did have a point. It was dangerous outside the wire. Most of the Iraqi soldiers had to provide their own transportation to the school. Some of the soldiers were offered rides with the military convoys down to the camp, but many of them refused. I assumed being seen traveling in an army convoy was more dangerous. The fact that they were not given weapons to protect themselves discouraged some from coming. For them, it was just too risky.

The missile and mortar attacks increased. The enemy had become somewhat successful at striking a few of their targets on both sides of the camp. Almost daily several buildings, vehicles and other structures were damaged, as a result. Some of the buildings had just undergone renovation. The militants frequently targeted Camp Taji, I questioned NATO's defense tactics. Not to say I knew any more than those calling the shots. I never attended a war college, but I thought simply beefing up patrols around the camp would help to decrease violence on the compound.

I was worried that one day one of the rockets might do real damage, resulting in the loss of life. I was uneasy with the Iraqi Army's rotation policy. The Iraqi soldiers would leave the camp every two weeks for a break from training. Getting the opportunity to spend time with their families, was their highest motivating factor. However, for the training team, it was like working with two different armies.

The interpreters had a similar system to that of the Iraqi soldiers. At times, the interpreters rotated more frequently than the Iraqi soldiers. They switched every seven days, different from the fourteen days on and fourteen days off system that the Iraqi soldiers were on. It was something that I never really adjusted too. It was crazy; every seven days I had to work with a different interpreter.

Sergeant Todd and I were working to complete an important project for Colonel Sam. He needed to present it to the generals back in the Green Zone. Rami was afraid that we would not take time out to escort him to the gate when the time came for him to rotate. "Hey Sergeant," Rami called out to me, with a grim look on his face. "It doesn't matter to me if we are in the middle of training, a meeting, or in the middle of a small arms fight. When it's time to go home and see my family, it's time to go."

Rami wanted to make sure I knew he was up for the next rotation, and for me not to find a reason to hold him back. "Sergeant Slade, don't forget that we have to pick up my paycheck, meaning we have to leave extra early." He wanted reassurance that he would be able to travel home to be with his family. He needed the cash to pay for the trip, as well as to support his family members.

Rami emulated the same mentality of most Iraqis whom I encountered on the camp. When it came time to rotate, they stopped everything. It didn't matter, they put everything that they were doing aside. They packed their bags on the eve of the rotation by jamming their personal belongings into their luggage. Afterwards, the only thing left was to wait until morning to leave. The Iraqi soldiers changed their uniforms and dressed in their civilian attire, hoping to conceal their identity as soldiers, as they prepared to walk out the main gate on the day of the rotation.

I found it quite interesting that the soldiers all came from different regions and ethnic groups. They remained loyal to their groups, regardless of their serving in the army. Sergeant Mohammed and Hani educated me on the various groups.

"Sergeant Slade, I bet you didn't know that we have more than 100 ethnic groups in our country." The Chief was happy to enlighten me on a little history about his country. The Chief was not a representative of any ethnic group. 'Chief,' was a nickname given to the highest-ranking Iraqi Non-Commissioned Officer on the camp, which he was at the training school.

"That's right, and we are more respectful to our brothers than to any government, or military organization," Sergeant Mohammed said.

I had no idea how to identify who was a member of what ethnic group. I asked Omar how I could distinguish the difference. Omar and Sergeant Mohammed gave me a short lecture on how to tell the difference.

"Sergeant Slade, you can tell the difference by their actions, and their speech." The more religious and conservative Sunnis, usually wear a black or white turban. Both claim to be more committed to their faith than the others. Still, they can live and work beside each other in a crowded city. "Take a look around

111

the school at the different civilian clothes that the Iraqi soldiers wear. If you watch how they dress, you will notice a difference. Omar said."

Being from a different ethnic group didn't seem to bother the Iraqis as they rushed towards the gate trying to avoid getting caught up in foot traffic. There was a mixture of nearly 400 soldiers who rotated every two weeks. I am not sure how anything militarily was accomplished.

Sergeant Todd and I were responsible for escorting the interpreters to the gate. That process included signing them in and out of the gate. Otherwise, they were unable to enter or leave the camp. Each local nationalist that crossed over to the coalition camp had to have a sponsor. The sponsor became responsible for their whereabouts and all their actions, during their stay at the camp. These rules applied only for the coalition side of Camp Taji. The Iraqi base had similar laws, but thank God that Sergeant Todd and I just had to deal with the coalition side.

The gate guards examined both the credentials and the bags of everyone that passed through the gate. The whole gate procedure lasted for at least an hour at times, due to a large number of Iraqis going in and out of the gate. Whenever someone left the camp another someone was coming. These checks were carried out nearly every day. Not only did the guards have to deal with the rotation crowd, but they also had to check in the locals who worked on the camp, as well as all the deliveries that arrived.

The gate guards were always on high alert, because of the frequent attacks by the insurgents at both the U.S. and Iraqi gates. More than once suicide bombers discharged bombs at the coalition gate resulting in the deaths of both Iraqi and American personnel.

That's why it was important that personnel going in and out of the gate underwent tight security checks. All items that they jammed into their bags had to be examined to ensure there was no contraband transported in or out of the gates. All credentials relating to the military was left behind in one of the mail slots inside the guard house. The reasoning was for safekeeping and to ensure that the Iraqis wouldn't be identified as, working with the coalition governments.

Some of the most dangerous incidents on the camp were carried out at the main gate. I was always apprehensive about going there. It was one of the most frightening places where I had to conduct business. Delivery trucks were left abandoned near, and in the parking area. The abandoned trucks had been riddled with bullet holes, and set a fire, by insurgents. I am thankful that no major incidents occurred during the many times that Sergeant Todd and I were at the gate.

12

There was a significant increase in violence throughout the heavily populated urban areas of Iraq during the month of October. Nonstop reports of bloodshed was reported by the major news outlets who were assigned to the region. Their aim was to make the world aware of the worsening conditions, and the scores of innocent lives lost during the first few weeks of the month.

Being surrounded by all the chaos, and not hearing any good news for days was emotionally draining. Then there were those frequent communication blackouts, that we experienced. The blackouts were due to the growing number of soldiers killed while out on patrol. More than once, the bodies of contractors were found dumped just outside the main gate on the coalition side of Camp Taji.

Those were some difficult times. I could not allow myself to become emotionally sunken by things that I had no control over. I searched for different ways to cope. One thing I found to be helpful with counteracting my emotional lows was journaling. Whenever I found the opportunity, I would write about everything, everything I saw, everything I heard, and everything I thought I heard. Sometimes I would sit for hours filling blank pages with words that had no significant meaning.

I wrote to escape from reality. Writing enabled me to transfer my emotions to paper. On many occasions when I would hear the explosions of bombs, rockets, and mortars, I would take refuge in front of the keyboard. The louder the noise, the faster I would pound the keys with the tips of my fingers, hoping to deflect the sounds of war.

I wrote on the computer, in journals and on scrap sheets of paper. The weightless paper became heavy with the words I used to describe my temperament of feelings. Transferring my emotions to words meant that I had less of a mental load to carry. Afterward, I would print out the papers burying them into one of my storage containers with thoughts of never having to view them again.

On the days I wasn't writing, I wandered around the camp investigating nearby points of interest. One particular place was the 'vehicle graveyard,' as it was called. It was a junkyard for all types of military vehicles that had been destroyed during combat, from as early as the 'Desert Storm' conflict. From there, I would eventually end up on the Iraqi side of Camp Taji conversing with the local nationals, and civilian contractors who could speak English. Those conversations were a mixture of sadness, happiness, and humor. I enjoyed listening to their amazing stories.

I spent a lot of my free time trying to understand the Iraqi soldiers, and what was going on inside their heads. I wanted to know how they felt about the continuing devastation that took place in their country. It was obvious that they were feeling more dispirited about life than I was. They were forced to live in their invaded country with their lives turned upside down. It seemed as if there was no end to their distressed lives.

Comparing the Iraqi soldiers' problems to those of my own, made it seem as if I had none. All the fighting, pain, and back-to-back wars had taken a toll on them. Foreign soldiers like myself were supposedly sent there to make their life better. My team did what it was tasked to do, however, I don't believe that we were totally successful. I predicted back in 2006, that for years to come, that the Iraqi people will be struggling to have a normal life. "Inshallah," as the Iraqi soldiers would always remind me.

Of course, Iraqi soldiers had mixed feelings over the presence of foreign soldiers in their country. A large percentage of Iraqis did not believe that foreign soldiers made any part of their lives better. It was likely that those that did, had some sort of connection to the coalition.

Because I spoke through an interpreter, I didn't feel that my true message was accurately being expressed.

"I like you both Sergeant Slade, and Sergeant Todd, you both are different, and have done a lot already for my people. But we are better without all the violence that came with you," The chief sergeant told Sergeant Todd and I, during one of the storytelling sessions that we had grown accustomed to having during chai breaks.

"That's true, as long as the Americans are here, things won't get any better. We want our old life back. Understand, that has nothing to do with you two guys. I just don't like what is happening to my country, and my people." Sergeant Mohammed said as he stood in the middle of the floor with beads of sweat running down his bald head.

Foreign troops weren't the only issue that divided the Iraqi people. Major differences between the Shiite and Sunni sects continued to contribute to the conflict. When the time was available, Sergeant Mohammed and the Chief would spend long periods of time going over the history of wars in Iraq with me.

The Sunnis were in the majority in most Middle Eastern countries, however, in Iraq they were the minority. After hundreds of years, the Sunnis and Shiites were still fighting for power.

"The fighting was not always as intense as it was during the period of 2003, up until 2006," the Chief said, while Hani translated.

The origin of the fighting began after the death of the Prophet Muhammad. Both the Chief and Sergeant Muhammed

told stories of religious wars dating far back in time. But neither was able to give me specific reasons for the current war.
Most of them were just short of blaming it on the invasion of
the Americans. They even brought up the fact the US had a
legitimate reason to be in Afghanistan and said that's where we
should have been all along, not in their country.

It was hard to be hopeful over the future of Iraq when
there were reports of people being beheaded and blown into
pieces nearby. September of 2006 took a toll on everyone in the
region, and it appeared that October of that year would be no
exception for both military and civilian.

Especially for those of us who were counting down the days
until we were to leave for home. "Hey Sergeant Slade, you're an
old man! You should not even be here. You, my friend, are a senior citizen. Senior citizens should be retired, and not involved
in a war," Omar said.

Omar and some of the Iraqi soldiers did not understand
how soldiers like me, were called up to participate in the
Afghanistan and Iraq conflicts. My explanation did not stop
Omar from poking fun over my "So call senior citizen status."

"Why would the Americans send old men to fight a war,
anyway?" Omar asked. "That's cra-zee!" he said laughing and
calling out Colonel Sam, and myself.

"It is rare that you see an old Iraqi soldier in a uniform, except the Chief, and he is a crazy old man himself," Rami added
as he was making jokes over age and war.

Their concerns for me became another motivating factor
for my survival. It reminded me of a poster I saw in one of the
recreation centers on the camp. There was a question printed
on the poster in bold red letters, that read, "Why are you here?"

I stared at the poster for a long period with mixed feelings.
Why was I here? How did I end up in a place like this?

Never mind how I ended up there, I was there and I had to
move forward. I was getting close to the midway point of ful-
filling my commitment. I wanted to keep my agreement with

the government, and I trusted that it would keep its agreement with me in the coming years. The government agreement that I was looking forward to, was my retirement pension.

Leaving Iraq to return home and settle down was something that I often dreamt about. But what happened next was no dream. I looked up into the desert sky and saw that bright orange ball of fire, had disappeared. It was mid-October. I will never forget those amazing images that were displayed across the Iraqi sky. The sky was no longer blue. Replacing the clear blue sky that I was accustomed to seeing, were large and scattered low hanging dark gray clouds. The clouds were blanketing the sky and floating freely and slowly across the upper atmosphere. Every day seemed repetitious up to that point.

It was hard to believe how fast time was passing by. It had been six months since I'd seen clouds in the sky. Everyone nearby stopped whatever they were doing. I took a seat in the chair outside my door to watch the clouds. A storm was truly on the horizon. The clouds were low and highly visible, depicting an entirely different image over the hot dry desert. Something different was about to take shape. For a short period of time, it no longer felt like the desert. The temperature dropped below 32 degrees Celsius, which is 92 degrees Fahrenheit. For that region, it was considered a little on the cool side.

The sounds of war came to a halt. Everything was still and calm.

Finally, there was peace, peace, and stillness, if only for a few moments.

It felt like home, on a warm day, awaiting the rain to fall.

Moments turned into an hour or more while I sat there anticipating the rainfall. After waiting and waiting, the rain never came. Eventually, nightfall crept in, and the clouds drifted away. The stillness faded into the darkness of the night sky. Although there was no rain, there was the joy of spending an evening of tranquility and stillness. I went to sleep very relaxed. After getting some of the best sleep I had gotten in months, I woke up the next morning feeling refreshed.

Two days later in the wee hours of the morning, I was awoken by what I thought was the sound of mortars and rockets exploding. The noises this time seemed to be coming from a greater distance. *Wait a moment. These are different sounds; ones I haven't heard here before.* It wasn't mortars or rockets that were being fired: it was thunder. I stepped out to look at the sky and I could see flashes of lightning. The storm was back, bringing along with it showers and the smell of freshness.

I jumped out of bed and ran out of the door wearing only my underwear, and began to dance in the rain. Suddenly I heard voices, "Hey, hey, it feels good." Looking in the direction of the voices, I could see the silhouettes of my nearby neighbors, dancing in the rain as well. We had all missed the rain.

I spent the next morning sobering up from a half day and night of emotional drunkenness, compliments of Mother Nature.

Given all the bad news of soldiers and civilians being killed during that fall season, a break away was badly needed, even if it only came from the excitement of dancing in the rain. I still had a lot to be thankful for, the most important thing was, I was alive.

I did not have a collection of heroic war medals on my chest, and neither did I have a lot of material possessions. People were dying all over that war-torn country. Most of the deaths that occurred were senseless, and without reason. Hearing constant sounds of heavy artillery cannons, and explosive bombs going off was reassurance in one way. The sounds let me know that I was alive, and I was thankful. To me that was more significant than anything else.

A day or two later when things returned to normal, I arrived for duty earlier than usual. It was already warm and the sun was up in full circle. Walking through the bright blue double doors, I was greeted by Colonel Tee in the hallway. He did not look like himself. Neither did he look like a soldier, let alone the Iraqi Commandant. He stood there with his thick dark hair, pointing in all directions. His eyebrows matched the shape of his hair. He was not wearing the shirt of his uniform and was dressed only in a white undershirt, and his chocolate chip 'BDU' trousers, and slip on sandals. I noticed the dark rings under his eyes, and he looked very disturbed.

Colonel Tee anxiously approached me and began speaking very rapidly. I was unable to understand anything that he was saying. "Sorry," he started over, slowing down his speech. "I have been up all night. I just returned from my home in Baghdad."

"Sergeant Slade, there was a rocket attack right outside my front door. It landed only a few meters from my home." I had never seen him that shaken and not dressed in his military attire. On most occasions he was an early riser, neatly dressed and proudly parading around the training school, with his military medals shining on his chest.

Colonel Tee believed insurgents had been following him and the rocket that landed nearby was intended for him and his family.

"I was up most of the night along with my neighbors. We were guarding our homes, trying to prevent more attacks. I do not trust the Iraqi police. I believe they were connected to what took place in my neighborhood last night."

Colonel Tee did not want to return to the camp, leaving his family behind in his atrocious neighborhood. However, he had a very important meeting to attend with one of the American generals from the Green Zone. So, before leaving home, he snuck his family out of his house and brought them to his brother's home, who lived in a safer neighborhood.

The BBC news media reported a story one day earlier about the distrust of the Iraqi police. The reporters detailed a few violent incidents that took place in which the Iraqi police fail to investigate, and how they were turning a blind eye to selected crimes. Reports also alleged that "death squads" were allowed to operate freely throughout neighborhoods and cities across the country, committing major violent crimes.

I discovered from listening to the BBC that the tally of civilian deaths in that one month was over 700 in Baghdad alone. That was an alarming number of deaths for one month.

"My brother, my brother!" Hani jumped out of the passenger side of Colonel Sam's small dirty white Nissan pickup truck, running towards Colonel Tee and myself. He was shouting to us that someone shot his brother outside his home. Colonel Tee and I stood there startled as Hani begin giving us more details of what happened.

Hani received a call from a family member telling him the news of his brother being shot earlier that morning. Apparently, his brother was shot for refusing to cooperate with terrorist gang members. Luckily local bystanders were able to rescue him and rushed him to the hospital. He was given three pints of blood; replacing the blood that he lost, and eventually, he was sent home. The wounded brother was not allowed to stay in the hospital, because the only room in the hospital was for the seriously wounded. That was surprising to me; I assumed losing three pints of blood was serious. It was well known to many throughout the community that hospitals were dangerous places. There had been numerous attacks on patients, resulting in many being killed while seeking treatment to stay alive.

Insurgents sought information on Iraqi informants throughout the neighborhoods, terrorizing its citizens. They worked mostly in safe havens they had established close to the homes of the Iraqi soldiers and civilians who aided the U.S military.

CNN international news reported that during the first 18 days of Oct, 70 American soldiers were killed in Iraq. There was speculation if the report was true or not. If the report was true, it had to have had a significant impact on all Americans. Especially those of us who were in Iraq. Those had to be some of the bloodiest days in the country. I heard another report on the BBC announcing that 10 US soldiers were killed in one day during the first week of September. That announcement was followed by reports that the Pentagon, and members of Congress were seeking a way out of the Middle East.

More violence flared up as clashes mounted between the Shiite militias and the Sunni rebels. Colonel Tee showed me pictures of some gruesome attacks that occurred around his neighborhood, the corpses of women and children who had been killed were left lying in the streets. Sometimes for more than a day, because the citizens were afraid to go out to remove them.

"Take a look Sergeant Slade, I took the photos while I was leaving the Green Zone, in a military convoy and on my way back to the camp. I am sad and ashamed of my country." The most gruesome photo was of kids playing soccer in the streets of Baghdad, one of them perhaps twelve years old was lying in a pool of blood in the middle of the street, gunned down by insurgents.

There were bad things happening all around me, but not physically to me. I knew then that someone was praying for me. As I reflect on that period of violence, I appreciated those moments of calm that were orchestrated by Mother Nature.

13

I woke up to news talk on my alarm clock radio. Before stepping onto the hard tile floor, I listen to the morning headlines.
There was nothing reported that was not previously known.
After listening for just a couple of minutes, I had enough. I got
out of bed and stepped outside to investigate my surroundings.
It was another morning after a very light rain shower. The brief
shower did little to settle the dust from the dry desert sand. Still,
any amount of water in the desert was appreciated.

Things were not going well for American personnel across
the country, in an attempt to boost morale among the troops, a
top US assistant general was scheduled to make his way down
to Camp Taji, that morning. All available U.S. personnel on
the camp were asked to attend the assembly, that was to be held
in the main recreation center. On the day of the general's visit,
I was working along with Sergeant Todd to complete another
project for Colonel Sam. We also had important logistics matters to attend to, around the same time that the visiting general
would be speaking.

Colonel Sam excused the two of us, from the assembly. Besides, I didn't think that we would be missing much. Attending
another war pep rally would not smooth over anything that
was happening on the ground. But, for some it was a nice social
gathering, giving some soldiers an opportunity to mingle with
those who they rarely got to see.

The "shock and awe" that some had been predicted, never happened. The general only gave a few hours advance notice that he would be visiting the camp. Just one day before his announcement, the camp was hit with 16 rockets. That was a lot of artillery hits for the camp in one day. To my knowledge, everyone survived without injury. But several buildings and a few helicopters were damaged. The camp was an important target for militants because of its location and the purpose of its existence as an aviation unit. Camp Taji, is 36 sq. kilometers, which is equivalent to about 14 sq. miles. It was a rather large camp, with most of the landscape being bumpy trails, and open desert.

It looked as though the attack got the attention of the top brass in the field. I knew very well that the general wasn't coming just to give a speech. I assumed another reason for him coming was to survey the damage done to the U.S. side of the camp. I wasn't knocking his timing for coming, after all that was his job. Besides that's what good leaders do, they get out in the field and lead when morale is low and things don't seem to go as planned. But many soldiers really didn't have the liberty to stop and attend the pep rally. Therefore, other than the officers, and higher-ranking NCO's, many of the line soldiers were not able to attend the assembly. Many were on patrol missions, and some were conducting normal operations that could not be stopped.

Once the assembly was over, the topic of discussion quickly made its way down the chain of command. It was said that the general reiterated "how proud he and the American people were of every one of us who were in Iraq fighting for the independence of the Iraqi people." It was nice that the 'Big General' came, but bringing words alone wasn't enough to end the violence. Neither did his comments about how bad of a man Saddam Hussein was. Honestly, that didn't matter anymore, because Saddam Hussein was no longer living, and his death didn't stop the violence. I didn't understand why his name was being tossed around anyway. I agreed with something that

Sergeant Mohammed, and the chief, said earlier: things were more screwed up after the death of Saddam Hussein than they were when he was living.

When the time came for Sergeant Todd and me to return to the main gate to sign Rami back in, it was a much longer process than normal. Security was rigorous, as the result of the Assistant Commanding General visiting from the Green Zone. We waited almost two hours while Rami went through a very strict security check. Rami was returning from his extended vacation in the city. He had lots of information that he wanted to share with us. Mainly, Rami was anxious to tell how badly the security around the city had deteriorated.

"Hey guys, I knew the general was on the camp. I heard people speaking about it at the city market. You would be surprised how much the local people know about what's going on military camps around Baghdad. People share all kinds of information about what's going on with the Americans. They are afraid, so they talk to one another."

Rami continued, "I didn't bring too much stuff back with me this time. I knew security would be high at the gate, especially today. My friend is a translator there, and he told me what was going on back at the camp," Rami said.

"Okay Rami," I said, "you and your friend are down in the city talking about what's going on back at the Camp, isn't that a perfect example of sharing confidential information? "I wanted to make him aware of how careless people are when it comes to keeping their mouths shut. "Loose lips sink ships," I explained to Rami, the meaning of that quote, and how dangerous sharing secrets could be.

It was likely that the Iraqis knew that the American General was coming to the coalition side of the camp as well. Apparently, they learned about his visit from sources that worked in the Green Zone. However, no Iraqis were invited. The group of Iraqis who I worked with really didn't care about the general coming down.

125

We stopped training for lunch and Salah, (Arabic prayer) but we continued the conversation in Sergeant's Mohammed's room.

"What can the general do? His speeches won't stop the insurgents from killing the citizens of Baghdad. They don't care about him, or what he says," Omar said.

"Oh yes, he's right; Omar is right guys," Sergeant Mohammed said, nodding his head in agreement as he laid out on the floor, with his hands joined together atop his round belly. He was either too hot or too lazy to stand. "Watch and see, nothing will change, same stuff will happen."

"It's almost like they want war," added the Chief. "I do wish it would all stop. Too many of my people are dying."

Sergeant Mohammed slowly lifted his head up towards the sky as if he was searching for clouds, as Omar translated for him, and couldn't stop chuckling as he translated. Sergeant Mohammed said, "It's okay with me if it rains every day. I have more faith in mother nature giving us a break from the violence than I do in the generals."

Then there was Rami, "You know guys, thinking about it, I sure do miss Saddam Hussein." Rami had said it a few times before. He like many others believed that the situation was not as bad when Saddam Hussein ruled. I listened, but could not agree because I really did not know the facts. Saddam Hussein did keep the insurgents under control and the warring factions. He himself still had people killed, but there were far less destruction and violence. I had been told all along that we American soldiers were in Iraq to liberate the Iraqi people from the harsh and brutal rule of law that Saddam Hussein governed by. But listening to those guys left me with moments of doubt.

I had to be careful and separate the fiction from the factual information.

"What do you think, Sergeant Slade, about your American general coming to the Camp?" Omar asked with a sly smirk on his face.

My answer to Omar was, "It's a good thing that the general takes time out to come down and visit the troops. Furthermore, that's how good leaders respond. It means a lot to soldiers in the field to have the top brass stop by. That is the utmost motivating maneuver any leader can make to his troops." Despite our differences, the Iraqi group and I were able to hold lengthy discussions on a matter of issues. However, I did not want the group to misunderstand my loyalty to my country.

Altogether, I didn't quite understand what they meant when they expressed their feelings about not having Saddam Hussein around. However, I did know that for many Iraqis, he was the only leader they knew. No longer having him around, affected the whole country. It was torn apart and became a very dysfunctional land. They did not have much confidence in his replacement, Nouri Maliki. Some cited that too much corruption took place under his regime. They also did not like the fact that Maliki was hand-picked by the U.S. to replace Saddam. But, on the other hand, there were those that were willing to accept the baggage of corruption that came with him, in exchange for peace.

"I can swear this to you, Sergeant Slade, Iraq will be a thorn in America's side for a long time to come." That was the chief's blunt message to me, translated by Rami with the hope that I would relay it to every American willing to listen.

"There's just too much violence happening and nearly everything has been destroyed." Sergeant Mohammed muttered.

Sergeant Mohammed, the chief sergeant, and the interpreters were split when I asked if they wanted the Americans to leave Iraq. Their opinions were similar to the Iraqi politicians. Some wanted the US soldiers to remain in Iraq for security reasons. As long as the Americans remained, many of the Iraqi leaders felt secure in their political positions. Their ordeal was similar to the American politicians back in the States, who were busy trying to maintain their own Congressional seats.

A campaign had been launched by President G.W. Bush in an attempt to convince the American people that the Iraqis would soon be in a position to take over their own security. The president said, "Iraqis will govern and will be able to protect themselves within 12 to 18 months." Being there, and living there, I saw a different image of the future. From working with the Iraqi soldiers daily, I had my reasons to differ with the president. It was hard to see them being ready in five years. The core of the problem was many of the Iraqi soldiers were not disciplined and lacked trust in their fellow soldiers and their government.

The fighting between the sectarian groups was just too intense for anyone to predict an outcome. Wounds were too deep to heal in terms of months. It seemed like every man was for himself. For example, I took a good look at Colonel Tee when new training aids arrived. Training aids were desktops, laptop computers, office supplies, spare parts for radios, writing boards, and the furniture that went into each classroom. The list could go on to include toilet paper and whatever other items that were needed to operate the school.

Colonel Tee conducted his own personal inventory of the items when no one else was present. I watched, as he gathered many items and locked them away for his personal use. Colonel Tee hid items in his secret hiding places within his sleeping quarters. He had no idea that I was watching him from outside the doorway. He moved around, trying not to be noticed by anyone, like a burglar, tip-toeing through his victim's residence late into the night.

Colonel Tee was not the only Iraqi soldier who misused military property. Hundreds of Iraqi officers and soldiers took advantage of the monetary contributions that the U.S. and its allies offered during the conflict. It was one thing trying to survive, but the abuse of property was something different.

Hundreds of young Iraqi men were signing up for the Iraqi Army. Most volunteered, while others were forced to join. If those who were forced to join fail to do so, they were threatened with jail time. A large percentage of those who volunteered did so for financial reasons. For them, it was the only way of supporting their families. Since the collapse of their infrastructure, they didn't have many other options to choose from.

Some recruits joined the military because there was a high demand for military goods on the black market. They did so to make additional profits by smuggling uniforms, boots, tee shirts, underwear, and socks onto the streets.

The Iraqi Army would allow anyone who wanted to enlist do so. Judging from some of the Iraqi soldiers who I came across, it didn't appear that many criminal background checks of any kind were conducted on new recruits. Hani said that some of the most corrupt individuals in the country were serving in the Iraqi military.

"Some of those Iraqi soldiers who attend the training school steal uniforms, shoes, or any other type of training aid that they thought that could get away with. They will take that stuff and sell it on the black market, making fast money," said Omar.

"Thousands of dollars are lost to corruption almost every day," added Hani.

Yeah, I believe you, if anyone knows anything about making fast money, it would definitely be Hani.

Hani would often say things, and rap tunes like, "I am a bad Muslim. I am the biggest gangster Muslim that you will ever meet on the streets of Baghdad." He would say these things in a joking manner, but in reality, he liked taking short cuts and making deals. I had to be very cautious of his actions when it came to purchasing training aides.

Two of the Iraqi soldiers' favorite items to steal were uniforms and boots. The most popular boot was the "Special Weapons and Tactical" gear, (S.W.A.T.) combat brown desert boot. As they lined up in long lines to receive their gear, they requested to only be issued the SWAT boot. If given another brand or style other than the SWAT boot, they would complain and insist that they are issued that boot. It was hilarious listening to the excuses being made. "The other shoe does not fit. I can't wear black leather boots, they cause problems for my feet. No, no don't give me that other boot," a small framed Iraqi soldier cried out. They made up some of the craziest excuses in trying to get the SWAT boot.

Word finally came down from the chain of command, supposedly from a source of intelligence, that the Iraqi soldiers were receiving large profits on the street for uniforms and boots. After being around Hani, I was not surprised by the news. However, I was surprised to learn how widespread the corruption process had become.

One would have assumed that the Iraqi commanders would have done more to prevent the spread of corruption on the camp. I thought the safeguarding of military weapons should have been a priority. Especially after they were turning up on the streets. Local reports indicated that Iraqi armed rooms had been broken into and weapons were taken. There were reasons to believe that the break-ins were carried out by insurgents who had infiltrated into the Iraqi army. The infiltrators had also broken into several old warehouses on the Iraqi camp. The old warehouses were left vacant and unguarded by the Iraqi army. It's likely that the insurgents knew about entering the warehouses long before the coalition forces knew.

Because Camp Taji was so large, once you entered the camp, you had access to go almost anywhere. Sponsors were supposed to be responsible for the foreign nationals, but sometimes they wandered off on their own. They could go wherever if there were no guards, or restrictions posted.

After driving the dusty and bumpy trails for only minutes, we came upon rows and rows of steel and clay buildings, with no other surrounding facilities near. The buildings were located a short distance from the main camp and were once used for military warehouses before the first Gulf war in 1990-1991. This area of the camp was not secured. There was no electrical power to any of the buildings, and each warehouse had at least 10,000 square feet. Seeing the warehouses from a distance was enough for me. The war ruins on the buildings were visible; they looked creepy from the outside. I had no desire to enter any of them. Colonel Tee told me that the warehouses were once favorite targets of NATO bombing raids.

Apparently, some of the buildings had not been entered since the first Gulf war. It was also alleged that a few of the warehouses were used to assemble nuclear weapons. Our departed former team members told us before they left that there were lots of old military treasures ordered by Saddam Hussein himself, to be stored in a few of the warehouses.

Those rumors led to countless treasure hunts by many young soldiers during their spare time. I was reluctant to participate in any of those unofficial searches. The treasure hunts were too risky. Especially after it was alleged that chemical weapons were once stored in them. However, those allegations did not deter the curiosity of a few younger soldiers. They roamed freely all throughout vacant buildings in search of a piece of military history, or some sort of souvenir.

Once Hani and I took a drive and passed the warehouses, he pointed out to me that they were inspected by the American soldiers during the first Gulf war. "The coalition soldiers spent days searching for chemical weapons and weapons of mass destruction. They found nothing, and afterwards the buildings were left vacant."

As more American soldiers arrived on the camp, the population increased twofold. That included both vehicle and foot traffic. Patrols both inside and outside the wire increased as well. The warehouses and the tank graveyard were popular spots to explore and take photos. There were hundreds of old tanks that had been destroyed in the first Iraq war, "Desert Storm" and some during Operation Iraqi Freedom (OIF).

Junk from previous battles was spread all about the camp, and there were ruins from aircraft, and destroyed buildings, located on both sides. The building that I had called home was on the coalition side of the camp. It too was run down, but somehow it was converted into sleeping quarters. Those of us who lived there were really lucky to find that place. Living there was much better than living on the Iraqi side of the camp, with little or no power. I also felt safer knowing that there were other American troops nearby.

But one evening as I returned from duty, I was given some disturbing news. The caretaker told my team members and me that we would have to move.

"Because so many soldiers coming, too many people on the camp. You guys move back with the Iraqi soldiers, this side for the American infantry," the Indian caretaker said in his broken English. "You moving, you make room for the American soldiers, okay?" the caretaker reiterated.

It was true that hundreds of Infantry soldiers came as reinforcement. However, the middle-aged caretaker must have forgotten that the three of us were American soldiers as well. He must have thought because we were only a team of three and that since we worked on the Iraqi camp we should sleep there too. In part, he was right. We were supposed to be living on the Iraqi camp, but for Colonel Sam, Sergeant Todd, and me it was too dangerous, as well as being inconvenient.

To pack up and move would have been another emotional low. I had gotten quite used to that place. Living there had become my refuge from the danger. Even the rocket and mortar attacks had become the norm. I'd gotten used to the sand fleas attacking at night, and the lizards that climbed the walls had become pets.

This wasn't home, but it sure felt good being settled down. Nevertheless, I always kept my bags "at the ready," meaning in the event I had to make a hasty move, I would be prepared.

The interpreters were sharing a room a few doors down. My battle buddy and I broke the news to interpreters that they should prepare to move as well. We all needed to find a place back on the Iraqi side of the camp. Without any emotions, the three of them did not bother to answer. Apparently, they had experienced moving several times before with the former team. Our original assigned place to live was on the Iraqi camp. Although we were expected to move, we followed the interpreters lead, we never made it a priority. More important issues were pressing. Whoever it was that wanted us to move, must have forgotten. The subject never came up again, we never moved. I never saw the caretaker again, until the day of our departure, when I had to return the key to my room.

I was relieved that I didn't have to worry as much about coming under attack by living on the coalition side of the camp. Due to a number of insurgents who were alleged to have infiltrated into the Iraqi army, I feared that eventually, something bad would happen. The thought of coming in contact with insurgents was very unnerving. On any given day I had no idea of who I was dealing with. Not to mention the nights that I drove alone from the Iraqi side of the camp back to the coalition side.

One night that I'll never forget was when I drove down the main road. The drive from the Iraqi camp to my room was about three kilometers. Out of nowhere, I came upon two men in the middle of the road. I assumed that they were Iraqis, but I was not sure if they were soldiers. They were jumping up and down, waving, yelling out in their native tongue. I was not sure of their intent, neither was I interested in finding out. I pressed down with all my might with my right foot on the accelerator, and using my right hand I blew the horn on the little Nissan pickup truck. That was my first and only warning for them to clear the way. I had no intention of stopping, and if they continued to stand in the roadway, I thought, whatever happened, happened. I did not want to cause harm to anyone, neither did I want to be harmed.

Eventually, the two of them jumped out of my way. My blood ran cold. The only thing I could think of at the time was maybe they were on a suicide mission, or that they were insurgents trying to sneak onto the coalition side of the camp. But I wasn't taking chances by exposing myself to danger. I was happy when I passed through the checkpoint on the coalition side of the gate.

The next day I was back at work and as soon as I saw Hani and Sergeant Mohammed I told them about my driving incident. Sergeant Mohammed couldn't stop laughing and informed me that, "Some of the Iraqi soldiers and interpreters hung out on the Iraqi camp late at night, and get a little crazy,".

"I don't like to be out at night, and you should never do that Sergeant Slade, come and get me to go with you. That's why I am here, to help you," Hani added.

Like so many other soldiers in the mix of war, all I wanted was to accomplish the mission and to leave. Sometimes, that involved working late. Progress was being made, at least with our fellow Iraqi soldiers. Still, I didn't see all the Iraqis meeting the standards as required. They continued to lack motivation when it came to working together. Lots of internal fighting continued as well. There was lots of work that needed to be done in order to get them to collaborate together. Without doing so, the Iraqi soldiers would never be ready to "go it alone."

I continued with my countdown to going home, regardless if the Iraqis were able to take over or not. I was ready to leave Iraq. I tried not to show my emotions, however, the interpreters, were well aware of my emotional ups and downs. They sometimes got a little emotional because of my emotions. They kept reminding me that a man my age should not be out late at night and in such a dangerous environment. They showed concern for my safety, which I appreciated. They knew I had a family and wanted me to be safe.

14

We had entered the month of December, and it was a little difficult not to think about the Christmas holiday that was only weeks away. The temperature was averaging around 75 degrees Fahrenheit, and the violence was ongoing. There were certainly no signs of a winter holiday approaching. Nonetheless, I knew the holiday would soon be here, and I had these despairing thoughts over missing Christmas with my family. At the same time, I had foolish thoughts; thinking that by some miracle, I could be home. I couldn't stop thinking of the variety of food that is usually cooked around the holiday season. I even imagined the aroma of some of my favorites, filling the room. Those were all fun times, especially when the family gathered, bringing with them lively conversations and lots of laughter.

Just before I could thoroughly entertain my thoughts, Colonel Sam and Sergeant Todd knocked on my door, presenting me with an early gift. Since the Colonel could only allow one of us to go home for the Christmas holiday, the two of them decided that I should be the one to go.

I thought it was some kind of a prank that the two of them were pulling. Often times one of them would make up stories about the unit being extended, or that we were leaving early to return back to the States. Most of the stunts they pulled were always about going or not going home. The pranks were another way for us to laugh in the face of the depressed and sad times that occasionally popped up. On that account, why should I have thought any different?

I'm not sure why I was chosen, nevertheless, I was excited about their offer. It's likely that Colonel Sam and Sergeant Todd had been discussing their plan for some time because they did not include me in their decision-making process. It might have been that they noticed my behavior and felt that something was weighing heavy on my mind. Colonel Sam was always telling me to chill out, and that I needed some R&R (rest and relaxation). Being away from home was already a challenge, and the back-to-back holidays of Thanksgiving and Christmas only compounded my sorrow of being absent from home.

I was happy that Colonel Sam and Sergeant Todd thought I should be the one to go home for the Christmas holiday. I was thrilled over the fact that they were allowing me to go. Although at the same time I did not want to appear as not having concern for neither one of them. I urged that they both reconsider and maybe it would have been better if one of them went. "The decision has been made, and you are the one going," Colonel Sam said, with that usual look of sincerity on his face. After the colonel amplified his voice and repeated the offer, I knew it was no joke. I thanked them both many times over.

As soon as the two of them walked away, I closed the door and jumped for joy. I felt like a bright cloud of happiness had replaced that massive dark cloud of gloom that had been hanging over my head. I will always be grateful to Colonel Sam, and Sergeant Todd for allowing me to spend Christmas of 2006, with my family. It meant everything to me, and there was no way I could repay them for the gift they gave me. Of all the soldiers to be deployed with, I was fortunate to be teamed up with two of the finest in the Brigade.

With the Christmas rush starting to go into full swing, I only had a few days before I was to leave for home. There was so much I needed to do before I began my journey. The day before I was to sign out of the camp, I took inventory of my belongings and secured everything of importance away in my wall locker. I really did need a break. I suspect the soldiers on the front lines needed a break more than I did.

There was no way I could sleep once I knew I was leaving—I was too excited—I stayed awake for 24 hours. I read, walked, and I did an extraordinary cleaning of my room. I did all of this while waiting for the time to arrive, allowing me to sign out on leave.

At the stroke of midnight on the 15th day of December 2006, I signed out of the unit and began my journey back to the states. There was no waiting for my flight out of Camp Taji since I had already registered for it earlier. I hopped a helicopter flight from Camp Taji down to the Green Zone. I was dropped off on the airfield. It was rigorous carrying my heavy army duffle bag, and wearing my battle rattle uniform. I was not yet out of the woods. It was still dangerous, but it was the only way I could travel. There was no other way out of Iraq.

After three dusty bus rides from the airfield, I arrived at the BIAP, makeshift military airport. During some point at the beginning of the war, the NATO forces seized the Baghdad International Airport. Within proximity of the airport, the US established a temporary flight operation center. It became the central hub for transporting personnel, equipment, and food throughout Iraq. The temporary airport was constructed with a mixture of large desert brown and white military tents made of thick canvas material and ¾ inch plywood for the flooring.

The entire set-up was impressive and carefully thought out. There were hundreds of cables that ran neatly across the floor and up the sides providing power and data to the computer systems. I was most thankful for the guys who installed the air conditioners; otherwise, there would have been more casualties as a result of the blistering heat.

Thousands of soldiers, contractors, and equipment passed through the temporary terminals daily. However, I was disappointed that I would not be able to get a flight out of Baghdad until late evening the following day.

I returned to the "stables," (code name) for tent city, looking for an empty sleeping cart to crash on for the night. I somehow ended up in the same tent that I'd slept in, on my first night in the country. Not much had changed in six months. The tents were still filled with unavoidable dust and a few non-working air conditioners. Like my very first night when I arrived in the country, I could hear episodes of sporadic small armed gunfire just outside the wire. This time things were a little different. I had grown accustomed to the sounds of war. I did notice an increase of tall concrete pillars that were added to the perimeter of the camp for extra protection.

After a much-needed shower to cool down, I flopped down on my sleeping cart for what turned out to be an uneasy night, with little sleep. I was too anxious about catching a flight, or the possibility of missing a connection for some unknown reason. I ended up tossing and turning all night, waiting for the morning to arrive. There were a group of soldiers nearby who were somewhat responsible for my loss of sleep, as they trampled on the gravel path just outside the tent. I could hear their desert boots crushing the gravel, all night long. The gravel route was a short cut for the foot traffic to the mobile toilets and dining tent.

The majority of the soldiers, doing the walking had probably just arrived in the country. Their first night probably wasn't much different than my own. They were likely experiencing jet lag and were unable to sleep. I presumed that they spent most of the night exploring the camp. Along with the newly arrived soldiers, were rotating shifts of guards who walked all night patrolling around the tents, searching for intruders, or any abnormal activity.

In spite of the foot patrol, I was a little wary of my surroundings, thinking back to my first morning in the country and being woken by gunfire.

It was a little before 05:30 and the sun had already risen and begun its journey across the Iraqi sky. With little to no sleep, I got up off my sleeping cart and rushed to get dressed into my uniform. I made my way to the temporary dining facility nearby in one of the large white tents. I had breakfast and was hoping to catch a flight to Kuwait a few hours later.

After a full breakfast meal, I went directly to the main operations tent and took a seat, and ended up waiting until late into the evening for my name to finally be called for a flight.

Hours later I heard the announcement. "Sergeant J. Slade, report to the main counter with your leave papers, and ID," a loud voice spoke through the PA system. When I arrived at the counter, I was told that there was a seat for me. The protocol was, active duty soldiers and soldiers with emergencies have priority. All others had to wait until a seat became available. Never mind how long it took, I was just happy to be assigned one.

"Your flight will leave in 45 minutes," a young female Air Force Sergeant told me after reviewing my documents. My dream of being home for Christmas was becoming a reality.

I received a seat on a large C-130 Hercules cargo plane, leaving from Baghdad going to Kuwait. I was thrilled to be going home for the Christmas holiday. I flew along with a few other soldiers and contractors, who seemed to be just as excited as I was to get out of Iraq. The senior military flight attendant asked everyone to take a seat and buckle up. I had already psyched myself for the uncomfortable woven cargo seat.

Being uncomfortable on the trip was not a bother. By all means, I was willing to tolerate the inconveniences that came along with the flight. Fortunately, the flight was only going to take one hour and twenty minutes. There was no wiggle room as I sat straight up, and bound to my seat. The plane had few passenger windows. The window nearest to my seat was blocked by two large cargo crates that were strapped down in the middle of the floor.

Moments after the flight attendants completed all safety checks, the plane sped down the runway, and was airborne. The plane didn't rise much higher than the clouds since it wasn't a long flight. All the same, the pilot elevated the aircraft high enough to prevent the plane from being hit from indiscriminate rockets that may have been launched by militants on the ground.

When we touched down in Kuwait, we immediately boarded the buses that were waiting nearby. The weight on my shoulders was much lighter. I was much closer to freedom than I had been in months. The chances of coming under attack, or something going wrong was less likely to take place in Kuwait.

"Okay listen up, everyone, you are now free to remove your battle rattle gear," the flight attendant announced. "Yes!" a small number of the soldiers cried out in sequence, and in harmony, as a sigh of relief.

"You may turn in your battle gear and your weapons to the armored storage facility to your right!" the senior airman announced, as everyone stood up to walk off the bus.

There were a lot of happy people in the crowd, and I was happy to be amongst them. After turning in my gear as ordered to do, I rushed over to the flight terminal to register for a flight to Germany. Slowly but surely and step-by-step, I was making my way home. When traveling with the military, there is a specific protocol that had to be followed. Including another mandatory briefing for all NATO personnel. The meeting was a reminder to be vigilant while flying in the Middle East.

The world was not a safe place, particularly for U.S. personnel abroad. Routine safety announcements could be heard broadcasting over the intercom system as the government tried to ensure that Americans remained unharmed, and updated on their surroundings. We needed to avoid traveling alone while wearing a uniform in certain places. It did not matter that we were not in Iraq, militants would launch attacks on Americans anywhere and at any given opportunity.

The briefings were a reminder for those of us who were traveling not to totally relax. No matter how routine, the briefings were necessary because there were too many hostile acts carried out around the world. It was up to all soldiers and citizens alike to be on guard for any hostile activity.

Once the last briefing was over, I was on my own. My attitude changed and my spirits were lifted. I surprised myself by whistling a few of my favorite holiday tunes while waiting for information on a flight out.

Finally, the announcement was made, "All passengers who are bound for Ramstein Air Force Base in Germany, please report to the departing gate. "

After the announcement, I jumped from my seat, grabbed my bags, and hurried to board the plane. I could not believe it was happening. I was on my way home, and to say I was excited, would have been an understatement. There were no assigned seats, and on that account, it didn't matter which seat we chose. I was just happy to board the jumbo C-5 Galaxy, one of the largest cargo aircrafts ever built. I had no problem flying on a plane loaded with cargo. At the time it was the only flight flying out to Germany, and I gladly took it.

Once all the cargo was loaded and one last briefing we were on our way. There was no opportunity to look out because the plane had few passengers windows. Having no window was no problem, because it was only a short time before the plane would land, and I would be inhaling the fresh air in Germany.

After a crew member announced, "Prepare for landing," over the intercom, those of us who were sleeping begin awkwardly shifting around in our seats, trying to wake up and recompose ourselves. I sensed that every passenger and crew member on the plane was just as excited as I was, that the plane was landing in a safe place—Germany.

Over the years, Germany had become my adopted home. I spent twelve years of my adult life there. For two of the twelve years, I worked as a civilian in the U.S. Embassy, assisting with security for U.S. personnel. The other ten years I was an active duty soldier, assigned to a Cavalry unit, in Bavaria for four years. The other six years I worked in a U.S. Army missile Battalion, that consisted of approximately 600 soldiers in southern Germany.

When I stepped off the cargo plane, for the first time in six months, I experienced real freedom again. Before claiming my bags, I rushed to find a phone to call my family to let them know that I arrived safely in Germany. I was not sure who was more excited, them or myself. But, I do know that I was nearly in tears. It was such a relief to be away from the daily mayhem of war.

A couple of hours passed before I was to board the next flight to Atlanta Georgia. I did not mind the wait. I spent a great deal of my military career waiting, whether in line or waiting for something to happen. I learned a lot about hoping flights, both domestic and abroad. Including were the daily flights that transported soldiers and other essential personnel, as well as logistics to Iraq. Patience was the key. I flew when a seat became available, occasionally it took a day or two longer, but it was cost-free.

I walked around the airport to amuse myself. I checked out the many shops, and along the way, I saw some of the things that I had been missing for the past six months. For a moment I felt a little odd. It felt different being back in a normal environment. I had become so accustomed to always being on guard, and waiting for something to happen. I stopped and stood still for a moment to survey the scene. Things were certainly different. People were walking around freely without worry. None of the things that I anticipated happening, ever did. Things were normal again.

Several soldiers were in the airport that day. Most of them appeared to be relaxed. They were not walking around in their uniforms, with all their battle gear attached. People were walking around conversing and laughing. From the look on most people's faces, it appeared that there was no worry of anything going wrong, like an attack by some radical extremist. It looked as though, that the only concern on the people's faces was catching their connecting flight. That was one thing I'd missed, being surrounded by normality and the sights and sounds of liberty.

Nevertheless, the one thing I did, was to take the security announcements in the airports seriously. I was vigilant of who and what was around me. This included being on the lookout for any foreign objects that might have been intentionally left lying around. As crazy as it may have seemed, I was overly precautious, and I probably looked a little weird to anyone that may have noticed me. Those tactics of survival were the results of all the training that had been embedded in my brain. I was afraid to drop my guard. Neither did I care to get too close to anyone or allow anyone to get too close to me.

I was startled by the next announcement that was made. It was almost as if what I was hearing wasn't real. However, the call to board the plane leaving for Atlanta was indeed being announced. Atlanta was almost the last leg of the trip. I rushed to the boarding gate to board the plane. A few minutes after taking my seat, I passed out, and nine hours later I was awakened by the pilot making an announcement for everyone to prepare for landing in Atlanta Georgia.

At last, I made it. I was back in the USA! Although I have not been gone that long, it felt a little strange being free to move about at will, without the worry of any security issues. After a two-hour layover in Atlanta, I reached my final destination, my hometown, Greensboro North Carolina. I never thought I would appreciate seeing vegetation as much as I did. I had been living in the desert for six months, and now that I had returned to North Carolina, I appreciated seeing even a single blade of grass, not to mention the extensive acreage of trees.

After walking through the long hallway of gates, I looked up and saw them; there they stood; the most important people in my life, my family. They stood there looking nothing like the last time I saw them, that was the day when I deployed. This time they were all smiles. We embraced each other with warm hugs, that symbolized our feelings.

Then the stories began, we had a lot of catching up to do. I paused for a moment before getting into the car, and uttered a prayer, thanking God for the day. Wishing that it would never end. I was in heaven, and I didn't want to think about returning to that land of chaos.

Being back home was an indescribable feeling. Never mind all the changes that I had gone through while I was away, nothing mattered more than those few days of joy. My family and I spent hours catching up on everything that we missed while I was away.

For some, six months does not seem like a long time. However, for me spending six months in chaos seemed as if it was everlasting. Within that period, my whole outlook on life was reshaped. I became more appreciated by the small things in life. One example was how nice it was to sleep in my own bed. For me, there was no other secure place in the world.

While lying in my bed, there were no interruptions, sounds of crushing gravel from soldiers walking by in the wee hours of the night. There were no IEDs exploding, or high-powered cannons being fired. Even the weather was on my side, the days were pleasant and sunny, and not unbearably hot. I relished the fact of being back in a relaxed environment. I was unmistakably at peace.

I was surprised to find that some folks who I ran into were concerned about my wellbeing, while others were only curious about the situation in Iraq. Some had no realization of what was happening there. Not wanting to be rude, but I let it be known that I didn't want to discuss Iraq while I was home. I only wanted to talk about what was happening at home.

But in spite of my wishes, some friends and friends of friends persisted that I give them my take on being in Iraq. A few of the elderly seniors, treated me as if I was their local hero. Not that I did anything special to warrant that title. They asked me to share my experiences with them. They had no idea what it was like to be in a war zone, or so far away from your family.

I respectfully answered most of their questions as best as I could. I made it clear that I was only expressing my personal views, and spoke only of my own experiences. I talked about the Iraqi culture, and the effects of the invasion by the American and NATO forces had on the everyday Iraqi people. I told stories of substandard, and dangerous living conditions that Iraqi families had to endure daily.

My friends and neighbors could have never imagined the hardships that the Iraqi people suffered. They had no idea how humiliating it must have been for a family to lose everything, and have no control of their future. I clearly wanted them to understand that the misfortunes that the Iraqi families experienced, were the results of their country being invaded. Their adversities were not the results of their own doing.

I did not want to talk about all the mishaps of war. I wanted to talk about the things that I'd missed the most while I was away from home. The things I missed were pretty ordinary. For example, just going for evening walks in the neighborhood, riding my bike, working out in the garden, or quietly sitting down to read a good book—all without the worry of being killed.

Those were things that I did not recognize with full worth before I deployed to Iraq. In just the six months that I had been away, I had come to realize how precious life was. I wanted those who prayed for me, to know how important they were to me, and that I loved each and every one of them. While home I wanted nothing or no one to interfere with the time I spent with my family. Being with them was so very important, that I tried to enjoy every tick of the clock with them.

15

There was only one day left before I was to begin my journey back to Iraq. I chose to spend it at home with my family. The last day home turned out to be a very somber twenty-four hours. The wait was everything but a day of relaxation. Preparation to leave was not like the first time. Even though I had spent six months in Iraq and knew sort of what to expect, leaving my home was still difficult. There was no certainty, and I feared the unknown. Leaving the comforts of my home, and having to return to the turmoil of war was not easy. Being in, and traveling around Iraq was dangerous.

I couldn't help but think about how my family might have been affected by my evolving moods during my last day. I tried to pretend that everything was normal, however, on the inside I was miserable. I spent most of the day trying to transform my mind back to that of a soldier. Nothing I did that day was easy. I could not keep my eyes off the clock as I literally watched each hour pass.

I was anxious about returning to Iraq, but at the same time, I was thankful I had the opportunity to come home. The worth of spending Christmas with my family was immeasurable in value. However, feeling grateful did not prevent me from wrestling with my thoughts of returning to Iraq. On the eve of leaving, I thought it would be better if only Thekla drove me to the airport. I requested to be dropped off at the entrance of the terminal, and I wanted Thekla to promise not to come inside. If my children would have made the trip with us again, it would have had an even stronger emotional effect on my leaving. I didn't think I could survive another episode of heart-wrenching goodbyes.

Ultimately, morning came, and I heard the last tick of the final hour on the clock. As much as I was dreading to get out of bed, I forced myself to get out. The time had come; it was time for the journey back to Iraq to begin the second half of my tour. Sticking to our agreement, Thekla and I left for the airport.

Things went smoother than the trip six months earlier. That's not to say leaving was any less easy, it was still difficult. It was discomforting leaving home, not knowing the future, or if there was even going to be a future.

After I was dropped off and goodbyes were said, I began the long walk through the terminal all over again. Like the first time, I did my best to avoid looking back.

Although I was halfway through my tour in Iraq, I wanted it to be over. I did not want to return, but I knew Colonel Sam, and Sergeant Todd needed me to fulfill my responsibilities. And more important than Sergeant Todd and Colonel Sam, I was obligated to fulfill the pledge that I made to my country. I knew I was going back to all the chaos, killings, and distrust—the whole country was dysfunctional. I was going from pleasure to pain, but I repeatedly told myself; I am halfway, I am halfway, it's almost over.

The passengers I passed appeared to be happy, as they made their way to their departing gates. I was very resentful, I wanted to be like them instead of being apprehensive over my journey back to Iraq. As a motivational boost, I spoke softly to myself, the job that I am doing in Iraq is one of the main reasons that the other passengers were able to walk around happy and free. That was just one of the mind games I played with myself, as I worked to mentally get back to the mindset of a soldier.

A nearby elderly couple must have sensed my misery. "God bless you and thank you for your service," the two of them said.

I thank them for their kind words, although I thought that if they truly knew how I felt, they would not just appreciate me, they would rescue me from my self-inflicted mental anguish.

I boarded the plane like a spoiled child and flopped down into my seat. At the same time, I felt a sigh of relief I made it that far. I tried to block out everything I heard or saw until the plane landed in Atlanta.

With less than an hour of being in Atlanta, I boarded the chartered military plane with my destination being Kuwait. Several hours later the pilot was making the scheduled stop in Ireland allowing everyone an opportunity to stretch. A crew was on standby to conduct a brief service check of the plane.

The thick clouds hung over the mountain tops, rivers, and the farmland. That was my one last chance to enjoy the images of nature and the beautiful green hills. It would be six months or more before I see anything close to it again. Iraq had its own form of beauty, but the destruction from the war ruined most of it. It could be open for discussion, but I think that no vision in Iraq came close to the beauty of Ireland. Like magic, and in a few moments, the whole scene disappeared. The images of the green countryside changed to brown.

I looked at the locator screen and saw that the plane was getting closer to Kuwait. I took a deep breath and held it as long as I could, trying to calm my anxieties. The pilot announced that we would be landing in Kuwait in about twenty minutes.

With a noticeable skip and a substantial bump, the plane's wheels made contact with the runway. The aircraft came to a screeching halt. I walked off the plane and boarded one of the transport buses that would drive us to the terminal, I saw a couple of soldiers and contractors that I flew out of the country with. They were also returning from their Christmas holiday in the States. Only this time they were not smiling. Instead, they looked subdued and dispirited. They appeared to be more business-like.

Those of us who had to retrieve our weapons and battle rattle gear from the warehouse were asked to remain seated, once we get to the terminal. The bus would take us to the warehouse, and the second half of my tour would officially begin.

I was back to dragging around my heavy duffle bag with all my battle accessories. Walking at a range walk, (fast pace) I made my way to the terminal. My search for the next flight to Iraq had begun. Unexpectedly, the helicopter traffic had slowed, due to the numerous attacks in recent days. I was unable to find any direct flights out to Baghdad. I had no other options, but to take a seat and wait. Hours went by, as I uncomfortably lounged in the terminal, watching and listening for any information on a flight to Baghdad.

The only flight that came up on the board that could get me back to Camp Taji was by way of Camp Fallujah. Fallujah was not the safest place for anyone to travel to. Reports of devastating assaults had been carried out there days before I left for the holiday, and continued up to my return. However, out of desperation and wanting to get back to my corner of comfort in Camp Taji, I took my chances and hopped the flight.

As the chopper got closer to Fallujah, darkness fell, it gave the radical fighters more confidence to come out from their hiding places. I knew that they were down on the ground hiding amongst the sand dunes. They used the darkness as a shield and would fire randomly at the aircraft. I don't know whether it was because of prayer or luck, or a combination of both, but we were not hit and eventually made a safe landing at Camp Fallujah.

I ended up spending a long restless twenty-four hours in Fallujah. I felt like I slept on two of the hardest plastic chairs ever made. I woke up early the following morning with neck and butt pains. All the same, and under the circumstances, I was thankful, that those were the only unpleasant things that happen to me while I was in Fallujah.

Getting a flight out of that place wasn't as easy as I was told. After my overnight stay, I finally got a flight and was on my way back to Camp Taji. It was already dark when the helicopter lifted off. The only visible light was the red dim and green lights coming from the instrument panels inside the chopper.

Two gunnery sergeants were assigned to protect the helicopter. Both were positioned on the left and right side of the aircraft with their window/door halfway open. The doors and windows were open for security reasons. Never mind that we were flying over the desert, it turned out to be one of my coldest flights ever. After all, we were in the middle of December, I should have anticipated a cooldown in the weather.

My eyes stayed on the gunners who aimed their 50th caliber machine guns down, and on two occasions they rapidly fired off a few rounds. Moments later, long tracers of gunfire and sparks shot from the red-hot barrels of the oversized machine guns. Expecting the worst; I gripped my seat and adjusted my posture, waiting to see what would happen next.

I trusted that the two gunners had everything under control. Seconds later my trust was gone. The helicopter jerked from a sharp maneuver that was made, causing it to momentarily lean to the left. From that point, I concentrated on everything that was happening. I had no idea what was going on, my heart skipped several beats.

The pilot compressed the throttle supplying more fuel to the engines, to elevate the chopper higher into the night sky. I could feel we were moving faster, and higher.

Thanks to the pilot's actions, the chances that the aircraft would be hit by the enemy fire were reduced. For the duration of the flight, I prayed that nothing would happen, and even more intense after the scare. Only a day or two earlier, I was home content, and grateful, now my life was suddenly back in danger.

Inside the helicopter, I assumed that it was too dark for anyone to notice my shifting around, and my spontaneous survival tactics. Looking down I could see what I thought to be rockets launched from the ground. Okay, what now? I asked myself, all while bracing for the next chilling maneuver.

One of the gunners must have noticed my fidgety movements through his night goggles. He signaled for me to relax and that everything was okay. Pointing to his watch, he indicated that a celebration of the New Year was taking place on the ground. I felt a little awkward and wondered what must have he thought of me.

Back at Camp Taji, I was an advisor, assisting Iraqi soldiers with training on communication equipment. I wasn't used to the type of warfare, and helicopter maneuvers that crew experienced during their many flights, almost daily.

Precisely at the stroke of midnight, the pilot gave us a jolting experience. Without warning, he shot off two rocket flares. "Boom! Boom!" two thunderous explosions were followed by two long colorful streaks of fire. The streaks were yellow and green and shot out from the gun barrels that were attached to the helicopter. "Happy New Year," the pilot said over the PA system. It was too late for me. By then, I was already in shock. It took several minutes for me to recover and appreciate the gesture.

Not everyone can say that they experienced a New Year's Eve flying over a war zone at the stroke of midnight. Yet there I was flying in a Chinook helicopter, over the most dangerous city on the planet. Compared to other celebrations, it was a pretty alarming and a once-in-a-lifetime event. I should add that it was one of my most spectacular New Years, to date.

A few minutes after midnight, the chopper touched down safely at Camp Taji. Tired and still hyped from my flight experiences, I finally made it back to my dusty room. Everything was just like I'd left it. I could hear explosions from outside the wire. I assumed that the local people were celebrating the New Year.

I was thinking of people all over the world celebrating the New Year, with their families and friends. But for me, I was all alone. There was no party for me, just sitting in my depressing dusty room, watching a lizard run about the wall. I let out a long, silent scream, with my hands raised in the air.

Why me, why me? Why was I the one who had to go through this? Why couldn't I have stayed home with my family?

The scream actually helped me to let go of my anxieties, and to accept things as they were. For the first time, I acknowledged that I was no longer myself. Something about me really had changed, but I could not pinpoint exactly what. I had never felt that way before. I felt that maybe being alone wasn't necessarily a bad thing.

I had to deal with a lot of irrational thoughts at the time, and only I could deal with them. I felt there was no one else around, who would understand or who would have time to listen. I knew there was a lot of work left to be done.

It took a lot of effort to find the energy to get moving. I laid in my bunk thinking about all that was going on in Iraq, and all the work that my team was doing. I wondered if we could really make a difference.

On the first morning of the new year, I slept until noon. The sleep was good for me, both mentally and physically. I woke up refreshed and deleted everything that occurred in my mind the previous night. I told myself that I could do this; after all, I was halfway. If I just get moving the energy would come.

Back at the camp, and a week into the New Year, nothing was different—it was business as usual. I wasn't getting much sleep at night, which wasn't good for my health. I tried to remain busy during the day, hoping that I would be exhausted by nightfall.

I decided to make changes and improvements. I would concentrate more on myself, as I began the second half of the tour. I needed to take a step back and reevaluate what I was doing. I tried to make a mental adjustment, as a way to hang on and prevent another breakdown.

As well as my angst, I'd been working hard with my team in seeing that the Iraqi soldiers succeed and become more independent. I didn't want my team to fail the mission that we were tasked to do.

I could not allow myself to take my eyes off the prize. The prize was a safe return home.

16

I realized that we were already in the second week of March. Outside it felt like July, with the temperatures soaring right around the 100-degree mark. I was glad the first two months of the New Year, were behind us. In any case, there were no significant changes in terms of violence. In general, for the past few months, every day was repetitious. Suicide bombings, roadside IED's, kidnappings and mortar attacks all continued, if not increased. By this time, I wasn't surprised that incidents of corruption were mounting, without resolve.

Corruption had become the main source of income for many. It was one of the few businesses thriving throughout the metropolitan areas of Baghdad. All things considered, I had absolute empathy for the economically poor Iraqis. Dealing in some form of corruption was the only means of survival, according to Hani.

"People are hungry, they can't just walk out and get food. They take a chance every time they walk out the door. Nobody is working anymore. What else can they do? May Allah forgive those who are only trying to feed their children." Hani made it known that he saw nothing wrong with conducting a few crooked business deals while trying to survive during the war.

I nodded merely agreeing with him. I don't think there were too many other alternatives for the poor, after losing everything but their life.

"I blame the war. The British, Americans, and the whole NATO, but not the Iraqi people." That was Omar's viewpoint on the subject.

As difficult as it may be for many living in affluent western countries to understand, I saw how living in a world of corruption was forced upon the Iraqi people. "People have to witness these conditions, otherwise they should withhold their opinion. I walk through the neighborhood and see nothing hopeful," as always, Omar was hoping to get the last word. The Iraqis certainly struggled to survive in an environment where their lives had been tormented.

It must have felt to them that time was at a standstill. Especially for those who suffered the most. All I could do was pray that things would change. One thing that was clear, time was passing. I reached a milestone. I was more than halfway through my journey which gave me hope. Although I was nowhere near being out of the woods. I was hopeful, but I was far from being relaxed, because potential danger still existed. I had a few months and days left in the country. My team members and I had a lot more work to do before we could completely turn things over to the Iraqi soldiers at the training school.

After almost seven months of being in Iraq, I was continuing to learn quite a bit about the Iraqi people. I learned a lot more about myself as well. Of those many awaken hours I laid in my bunk at night, many were spent pondering my own life. Up to that point, I guess I had done the right things to survive. It had not been all easy, I had to figure it all out. There were many ups and downs, some more stressful than others. It was war.

There were constant reminders that the war was not over. Like those constant booming vibrations traveling through the air. They didn't go away, and I had gotten so used to the sounds, that they became the norm.

One inconceivable turning point that happened one morning in March, was an incident that almost changed everything about my entire deployment. I was in the gym finishing up my routine fitness workout. There were about a dozen soldiers in the gym that morning. I'd consider that to be a fair amount for 0500 in the morning. Everyone was about to wrap things up and prepare to face the day's challenges. Just as two soldiers and myself approached the door to walk out, there were two awfully loud booming sounds.

We did an about face and walked back into the building for cover. One after the other some type of projectiles were being fired from nearby. "What was that?" One of the soldiers yelled out. All but two in the group were newly assigned to the camp. It was their first experience coming under a rocket attack. They nearly freaked out. However, it was one of the worst episodes of rocket attacks that I had experienced as well. Never had I heard a blast from a rocket so loud and clear.

The projectiles landed extremely close to the gym. The entire building shook on more than one occasion. It felt as if it was coming apart. The sounds became more frequent, growing louder and louder.

We all stood frozen in place and in silence, staring at each other. We were in total shock. Everyone waited to see how the guy standing next to him would react. We did not have any of our battle rattle equipment on hand. We were dressed in our gym clothes. Although we did have our small arms weapons nearby, they were no good for stopping sailing rockets.

After the noise stopped, we waited for about five or ten minutes before going out to survey the scene. The rockets landed in the military junk graveyard, about 90 meters away. Added to the scrap metal from the old vehicles, were about a half a dozen smoking rocket shells. The thick black smoke billowed high up into the already scorching sky.

The junkyard was located beyond the barracks and the gym. Landing that close, was convincing enough for me to believe that our housing unit was the target. This was the closest that any rocket had come to our compound since my living there.

Most of us were thinking the same thing. We were all in agreement that it was likely an inside job. We assumed that someone working there had given the exact grid location to the enemy. Every time there was an attack on the camp the local nationals were suspicious, including the interpreters. With regard to interpreters, many of them had close relationships with their counterparts. In spite of their close relationship, when the interpreters were back home on their days off, no one was aware of their activities. When bad things happened, and out of frustration, some soldiers allowed bigotry to play a role in their judgment of others.

Given that there were many interpreters and contract workers, it was difficult to really pinpoint exactly who was responsible for the rocket attacks. On the other hand, it may have been a stroke of luck that the rockets landed so close.

After things settled I return to my room. Once inside I examined the walls for damage and it appeared that everything was in order. I was thankful to be alive after experiencing a near hit from a rocket attack.

Minutes went by and I was still wearing my training shorts and a tee shirt. Things took a turn for the worst. I started experiencing sharp pains on the left side of my chest. The pain radiated all the way down my left arm to my hand. I fell across my bunk. I moaned, the words 'heart attack.' There was no one near to help. I thought this was the end of life for me. Images of my family flashed before me. For the first time in Iraq, I was really afraid.

I was all alone in my room. I knew what I had to do. First, I had to calm myself down. Next, I had to save myself. I eased up and gently walked out the door. I made it to the little dusty Nissan truck and calmly drove myself to the medical station about half a kilometer away.

I remained cool and explained to the medical assistant my symptoms. From that point, I became a priority. Two doctors came in and told me to lay on the examining table. They asked a few questions and at the same time, they placed a nitrogen tablet underneath my tongue. They did not waste time, they ordered an emergency helicopter ambulance to fly me directly to the military hospital in Baghdad.

When I initially went to the clinic, I had no idea that I would be medically evacuated to another facility. I went into a little bit of a shock. Despite the scorching temperature outside, I was shivering cold. After all, I was only dressed in my shorts and tee-shirt.

When they escorted me to the helicopter, they gave me a thick green wool military blanket for warmth and a helmet for protection. There I was dressed in fitness shorts, tee shirt, and wearing a helmet. That was quite out of line.

In no time we were airborne. I looked down at the sand dunes seeing activity and some movement. This time I was not really concerned with what was going on below. I knew the two gunners were in a position to handle any enemy activity we might have encountered. I was only concerned about my health, and nothing else mattered.

Moments later we were landing at Baghdad's Military Hospital. I was placed on a clean gurney and rushed into the emergency room. A few members of the medical staff greeted me assured me that I would be okay.

"Sergeant Slade, you are in good hands, and we will take excellent care of you."

Seeing my body trembling, one of the female military nurses held my hand. She sensed that I was afraid and wanted me to relax. I was heartened by how they responded to my medical needs. Their kindness showed me that they were sincere and cared about me.

"I promise we will not leave you alone, we are all family here." She assured me that I would be okay. Hearing someone speak words of kindness, had more of an effect on me than any of the dosages of medicines that were given to me.

I laid there with an IV plugged into my arm, which was at times uncomfortable. However, whatever was dripping out of it was keeping me calm. I underwent several tests as evening set in and I started to feel a little better. I could tell by the numerous times a different staff member came to my bedside, that there was a concern for my condition. One of the nurses informed me that I would be staying overnight.

"Sergeant Slade you will be reevaluated in the morning, and from there the doctor will make a decision on your health."

I was rolled to the elevator and up to the second floor. I was assigned to a semi-private room. There was already another patient in the room. A man with shiny black hair and gray streaks was lying in his bed reading a local newspaper. He was wearing two gold necklaces around his neck, and matching bracelets around both wrists. Unlike me, he wasn't wearing a typical hospital gown. He was wearing black silk pajamas with gold trimmings around the collar and sleeves. After I settled down he introduced himself.

"I am Mohammed." There was no need for an interpreter to communicate with him. His English was fairly good.

I introduced myself as an advisor from Camp Taji.

Mr. Mohammed explained to me how he got there. He said he had been riding in an automobile that was singled out of a military convoy and ambushed.

"I received wounds in my abdomen and upper right chest," speaking tenderly to avoid causing pain.

Where are you from? Expressing my curiosity.

I wanted to know more about Mr. Muhammad's connection to the US military since he was a patient in a military hospital. "This is my country; I am Iraqi from Baghdad."

Just as Mr. Mohammed started telling me about himself, a notably attractive female walked into the room wearing a beautiful tan dress with a matching hijab. She wore a large gold necklace, with one single diamond, dangling from around her neck. She was escorted by two large Arabic men dressed in black suits. She was there to visit Mr. Mohammed. I was certain that they detected my look of curiosity.

"This is my wife Sir." speaking directly to me, Mr. Mohammed introduced his wife. She only acknowledged the introduction by blinking her eyes twice and looking downward. His wife avoided direct eye contact with me. She wasn't being rude, I recall Rami, saying that it was customary for a female Iraqi not to make eye contact with a stranger. Mr. Mohammed did not introduce the two men in the room.

Mr. Mohammed's wife and the two men were only in the room for a short while. My suspense grew and, I was more interested in knowing who Mr. Mohammed was. Obviously, he must have known that I was curious when he turned and looked at me.

Going back to our earlier conversation, he said "I am the Iraqi Finance Minister and the two men with my wife are my driver, and her bodyguard. Security has been increased since the attack on my life."

Still speaking gently Mr. Mohammed told me, "I did not want to go into Baghdad's Main Hospital, for fear of my life. I do not trust the doctors for fear that they would kill me. Coming to an American military hospital is a secret, and safer."

I knew that there was something suspicious about him when I first saw him. After hearing his story, it all made sense.

In my mind, I questioned the reason why I was put in the room with such a high-profile diplomat. Although I never found out the reason. I assumed it for reasons that my stay in the hospital was just a little over twenty-four hours. The doctors decided that I would have to undergo more testing. As a routine practice and to be sure that I was not at risk for future problems.

"Sergeant Slade, the doctors made a decision to medivac you to a military hospital in Germany, for further testing." A nurse came into the room and informed me.

Still wearing a hospital gown and with an IV stuck in my arm they were preparing me for the evening flight to Kaiserslautern Germany. The medical staff did not waste any time. They were extremely professional and from my experiences, they did an exceptional job.

One of the nurses came into the room with gray sweatpants, a matching shirt, and a jacket for me to wear during my flight.

"Put these on, they are warmer than the clothes that you are wearing," she said.

Thank you so much. These are exactly what I need. I had done enough flying to know that the temperature on most military planes is set very low, it almost feels like freezing.

Hours later, I was discharged from the Baghdad hospital. I said goodbye to the Finance Minister, wishing him well and a speedy recovery. On my way out, I told him I felt honored to be assigned as his hospital mate during my stay.

Two of the nurses who cared for me rushed me out to the helicopter pad. There was one more stop before I was to board a plane for Germany. Once again, I was on the move. Things were not like back home, where you call a family member or friend and alert them of your situation. I was not even able to call my battle buddy. The kind nurse back in Baghdad said she would file a medical report notifying my commander back at Camp Taji. It would have been nice if I were able to talk to him myself.

The medical helicopter landed at Camp Ballad were several other medical evacuees were waiting to board the next flight to Germany. The noise from the huge C-17 Galaxy was unavoidable. The very large C-17 was a flying 'Triage unit' and were able to accommodate dozens of wounded soldiers. The bunks were stacked in doubles along the sides. There was also a special intensive care section where the air pressure could be regulated for the more seriously wounded.

One by one we were loaded onto the mobile medical unit. We were strapped on gurneys that we would remain on until we reached the hospital in Germany. Soldiers were carried to the plane according to the seriousness of their wounds. The seriously wounded were loaded first.

I was surprised to see that all the medical staff on the C-17 were all uniform military personnel, and they were very professional, as well as polite. They did their best to ensure that the passengers were as comfortable as possible. They also assured everyone that they were in good hands.

After the plane was airborne everything went as smooth as possible. Lucky for us we did not encounter much turbulence. I was really appreciative to be in the hands of such well-trained personnel. That goes for the pilot and all the crew members.

Looking around I saw some badly wounded soldiers. Some were hanging on for dear life. There was a young female who was severely wounded in her abdomen. She appeared to be the same age as my daughter. It broke my heart to see her lying there suffering from her wounds. I wanted to change places with her. I wanted to be the one lying in her place with my abdomen blown open. She was too young to suffer. A nurse held her by the hand during the entire flight.

Another young sergeant a few bunks down was badly wounded and in pretty bad shape. He appeared to be in a lot of pain but was able to speak. I overheard him saying that he was in a gun battle with militant radicals and was shot six times.

"The militants dumped me in a small canal and left me for dead. Luckily, I was able to crawl to the banks of the canal, where I was found by a patrol nearby." Although the young sergeant was in a lot of pain, he was lucky to be alive.

A Lieutenant General from Fort Hood Texas was accompanying us on the flight. The general was returning back to the States after visiting Iraq on business. He took time out to walk through the triage unit, thanking everyone for their service and for their bravery. He recognized everyone by presenting each one with a medal honoring us for our contribution to the country. When he reached the severely young female soldier and the young sergeant, he presented them both with impact purple hearts for their dedication and bravery. The general's actions were exceptionally symbolic and emotional.

Finally, we arrived at 'Landstuhl Military Hospital' in Germany. All the way up until the moment the plane landed, the medical staff continued to show their professionalism and hospitality.

The moment the plane came to a final stop, a ground crew was in place to transfer the medical passengers to a medical bus that was waiting nearby. We were taken to the hospital just over 300 yards away. When the bus arrived more staff members and volunteers were there to greet us including the hospital chaplain. Again, they pledged their support and thanked us for our service.

Still strapped into the gurney, we were unloaded from the medical bus, rushed into the large emergency room. I was looking around for the young injured female soldier. I never saw her taken off the bus or plane. I do recall seeing one gurney passed off the bus, with a white cover over it. It was placed inside a small van. That explained my not being able to account for the young female soldier. I don't believe she made it.

The belief I had about the young female soldier was true. Word had spread among the passengers in the emergency room that the young female did not make it. It was very upsetting to find out that the young female soldier did not survive. The chaplain called for a moment of silence, in her honor.

Nearly a half hour later after being processed in, I underwent another examination before being assigned a room later that afternoon. Two nurses came in and drew blood for the lab. Moments later I met with my assigned doctor.

In my room were three young wounded soldiers who had been there for a few days. The room was not a dark depressing gray in color with stone floors and walls like the one back in Baghdad. The room in Germany had an updated look. It was

163

painted a bright yellow with white trimmings and large glass windows. It was designed to lift the patient's spirits.

I finally got the opportunity to call home and tell my wife all about my adventures, and how I ended up in Germany. I made it clear to her that I was going to be okay, and not to worry. Besides, I was in a better place, than Iraq.

I waited three days for all test results to return. In between waiting, I continued to process into the hospital. I was put into a category that removed me from a combat zone, and into the medical holding category.

The chaplain and a few volunteers ran a small store located in the hospital. There were numerous items on hand in the store at no cost. The store was supplied by major retail outlets from all across the United States. The shelves were full of outer clothing, underclothing, toiletry items, notebooks, writing paper, and backpacks. Everything in the store was complementary of the 'Wounded Warrior Project.'

Having support from home was appreciative. But the overall objective of the hospital was for everyone to receive the best medical treatment needed and to be discharged totally satisfied. Never mind that we were patients, those of us who were able had obligations to fulfill. We were still soldiers and were not allowed to sleep all day. There were certain expectations and requirements of us all. We had to attend all scheduled appointments, educational classes, regarding healthcare and family services.

On the fourth day of my stay, as soon as breakfast was over a staff member came into the room and asked if we would like a visit from a VIP who was visiting troops throughout Germany.

Because it was Saturday I wanted to sleep in, and after all, it had been a stressful week. The staff member stood awaiting an answer. I asked who was the VIP? She answered with a smile on her face, and said so proudly "It's the Senior Senator from Arizona. He's running for President of our great country."

Without hesitation, I replied, Oh no, not me.

I have no interest in receiving a visit from someone for their own political gain. No, I would rather sleep in, if you don't mind, and I laid back pulling my covers up.

All three of my young roommates sat straight up in their beds with a look of surprise, to my response. "Sergeant, you can't say that. You can't refuse a visit from a VIP, especially a Senior Senator," one of the young soldiers said.

I answered the younger soldier by saying, he's only here because he's running for President. This would be the perfect photo opportunity for him. I am sorry, but I rather catch up on sleep. I am here for my health and not politics. However, in hindsight, and with respect to the late senator, I have some regret for not welcoming him into the room. More importantly, I really was concerned about my health.

Some 30 minutes later after I refused to play politics a nurse came into the room and told me that I was being discharged. Discharged? I asked using my loud voice.

Where am I to go? I am in Germany! She smiled, "everything has been worked out, you are being reassigned to the transit barracks in nearby Kaiserslautern."

I was to take a bus to the barracks along with a duffle bag of all my newly acquired clothing and toiletry items. Once I got there, I found there were several other wounded soldiers assigned.

I was briefed on the rules that we were to follow while staying at the barracks. Each day two formations were held for accountability. Along with that, I was required to make all scheduled appointments. Like all others I had to be in uniform during business hours.

Entering my newly assigned room, I notice two other wounded soldiers already assigned to the large room. Each one was assigned a bunk and a wall locker for storing their personal items. I immediately recognized one of the guys in the room as the sergeant from the medical airlift. He was the recipient of the Purple Heart. Seems like we were all acquainted in some way.

It looked as if no one in barracks laid around nursing their wounds or feeling sorry for themselves. All of those who were able were on the move, doing their own thing. As soon as the evening formation was over we were free to wander as we pleased, even into the city wearing civilian clothing. Being in the transit barracks wasn't a bad deal after all. It was much better than being in the hospital. It was a break from the war. It was freedom, something that we all needed. In contrast to Iraq, Kaiserslautern was a vacation resort.

That's exactly what we all needed. I also understood the importance of morning formation. Some of the guys got a little too loose at night and needed a little guidance and account-ability. Freedom from the war certainly affected each one of us differently.

For example, right after the last accountability formation of the day, everyone went their own way. My roommate with the six bullet wounds asked me to help him get dressed, by putting on his shirt and jacket.

Where do you think you are going? Without hesitation or shame, he said: "I am going to the Gasthaus to have a few beers." The poor guy could hardly walk, yet he was going out on the town with a few other soldiers.

I guess going out on the town was the part of being a soldier that I had long forgotten about. The barracks was nearly empty until about 2:00 AM when everyone started to return.

We were all offered a four-day pass and could actually leave the area. I was lucky to be in Germany for a break. I called and made plans to visit friends in the southern part of Germany, where I had spent close to twelve years of my life. I took a short trip to spend four days with friends. While there I was able to eat home cooked meals each day. I slept in the same apartment that I lived in for four years. Being in Germany was sort of a homecoming for me. The short trip was a personal endowment.

Most of the soldiers who were on pass all returned about the same time and late at night. I made it to my room and unpacked my new backpack and a few items that I picked up from the wounded warrior's store. I showered and jumped into bed, knowing that I would have to see my doctor early in the morning.

Shortly after midnight, I heard someone fumbling around with keys at the door. It went on for almost five minutes before I got up to take a look. It was my roommate, the sergeant, the wounded one, the one with the six bullet holes. He was wasted! Poor fellow, he couldn't open the door, and could not even walk. There he was half sliding, half crawling into the room. He finally made it to his bunk where he eventually passed out.

Morning came and we all made it to the accountability formation, even the sergeant. It was time to get back to business. We loaded the buses for a trip back to the hospital. I saw my doctor, and he gave me a complete exam. He had a few concerns and recommended that I should see a cardiologist.

Within a week, I was able to see the cardiologist, who eventually discharged me from outpatient care. Then it became decision time. "From this point, it's up to you. I could arrange for you to leave and fly back to the States, or if you think you will be okay, you could fly back to Iraq. However, there is still some concern," said the doctor.

It was entirely up to me. I could walk away from the war; go back to the States, return to my life, and be with family, and no more Iraq.

That was one of the biggest decisions that I had to make in my life. It was all left up to me. I could return to the comforts of home, and be surrounded by family and friends, or return to war and put my life back at risk.

I was given a few days to think it over. I thought long and hard during those few days until I finally was able to come to a decision. I decided to return to Iraq. I only had a few months left and I had already invested so much of my life serving my country. I wasn't exactly sure if my effort towards the mission was working but I wanted to fulfill my contract and serve out my duties. I started out my career as a soldier more than twenty years earlier, and I wanted to end my career without any drawbacks.

I told the captain in charge of the holding unit in Kaiser-slautern that I wanted to fly back to Iraq. She asked, "Are you sure?" I said yes, I was ready to go. It was a little different this time. I knew what challenges that were ahead, and again I psyche myself up for them.

Two days later I was on a military C-5 Galaxy cargo and passenger plane, flying back to Baghdad. I was flying among newcomers like I once was. It seemed like it was seven years earlier, but actually, only seven months had passed. Looking at the faces of the newcomers, I probably knew how many of them were feeling. Flying halfway across the world, going to war is one of the most difficult flights for anyone to have to take. But, there I was doing it all over again, and this time it was my decision.

17

After spending an entire month in Germany, and making the decision to go back, I was finally on my way. Despite my volunteering to return, the trip was nothing to be excited about. More or less, I wanted to return to complete the mission. My only desire was to make one final pitch to help the impoverished Iraqi soldiers whom I had started to miss. At this point, my team members and I had established a strong bond with the Iraqi soldiers. I didn't want to just disappear without saying goodbye.

As soon as I stepped off the aircraft and placed both feet on the ground, I was welcomed back by that gigantic ball of sweltering heat. The sky was as blue as the waters of the Arabian Sea. But then there were massive clouds of black smoke billowing up from a nearby burning oil field. The earth was shaking underneath my feet from the after-effects of a cannon that had just fired off an explosive artillery round. I was back and this was just a typical day in Iraq.

I reached Camp Taji and reconnected with the people that I'd left four weeks earlier. They were both happy and surprised to see me return. My team members didn't understand either, they thought for sure that I was on my way back to the States.

"Ha, ha- you came back. You're a crazy man!" Hani said the moment he saw me.

"Yeah, Sergeant, something wrong with you," both Omar and Rami said simultaneously.

I had worked with those guys since day one, and they thought that they knew me a little. But, not one of them expected to see me return. Nevertheless, they were happy that I did. More importantly, they were delighted that my health was better.

It was surprising to hear everyone say that they didn't think that I would return. No one believed that I would step back into Iraq. In spite of what the group thought, I came back. Which was like reading a novel, there was one last chapter left before it would be complete.

On my first day back on the job, I attended a meeting with Colonel Sam and the Iraqi commander. The topic: the transition plan. As a team, we were preparing to officially place all significant military operations back into the hands of the Iraqi soldiers. The biggest news I took away from the meeting, was that our original date of departure was extended some twenty days. For some, twenty more days in Iraq would be like an eternity.

But why was I complaining? I volunteered to return, along with that, I should have been well aware things are forever changing in the U.S. army. No one could ever organize or adequately plan for anything. As the Iraqis would have said to the situation, "Inshallah" (if Allah wills it).

More important, I was still alive, and my health had been given the green light. My days in Iraq were numbered. I had reached a point where I could almost see the light at the end of the tunnel.

I returned to Iraq just in time to celebrate my 50th birthday. For years I had planned to celebrate with family and friends. Unfortunately, due to the conditions and the environment in Iraq, there was no special celebration. Instead, I acknowledged the fact that I was alive and that I reached that milestone.

I ran five miles on my birthday around the camp, which was good enough for me. I did take the advice of the medical professionals and listen to my body. I didn't want to overdo it and have to experience another medical evacuation like one-month earlier. But I did enjoy running, it allowed me the time to focus on me. That was one of the two things that worked well for maintaining my mental stability, the other was writing. I did whatever I could to turn negatives into positives.

Daily changes were constantly being sent down from the Green Zone. The members of the unit were under tremendous pressure to complete all tasks as the time for the transition was approaching. As the days on the calendar got down to double digits, I avoided going down to the Green Zone for anything. The situation there was risky because the area randomly came under attack by militants. Patrols were beefed up throughout the city of Baghdad as an attempt to decrease the violence in the neighborhoods.

Never mind all the extra security that was brought in, it did nothing to halt the attacks. My team members and I worked long and hard to ensure that the Iraqi soldiers who we had been working with for ten months, were capable and ready to take over for themselves.

One U.S. male soldier and a female contract worker from the U.S. who worked with the KBR outfit were killed by a random act of violence. The two of them were enjoying leisure time sitting by the pool down at the Green Zone when they were hit by a rocket. I had visited that pool on two different occasions. Both times in October of 2006 to take a break and get a little R&R. The pool was a great place to hang out for soldiers. Occasionally many after-duty parties were held there.

Traveling around the country back then was just not a good idea. The days I had left in Iraq were getting shorter. However, there was still enough time for something to go wrong. I wanted to play it safe and not take any risks. If traveling was not a priority, I didn't do it.

To play it safe I spent most, if not all of my remaining time on Camp Taji. Sergeant Todd and I hung out with our Iraqi comrades carrying on after-duty conversations. The funniest was when Hani, talked about a comment that he saw on CNN referencing the late Senator John McCain of Arizona, and President George W. Bush. They both declared that it was safe to walk through the city of Baghdad, without protective gear. Hani, Rami, and the group of Iraqi soldiers all exploded with laughter.

"Yeah, tell the two of them to come to walk in my neighborhood!" Hani said while still laughing. "They will see just how safe it really is."

"No, tell them to walk through *my* neighborhood," Rami said. "My neighborhood is worse than yours Hani."

Omar, the Kurdish interpreter, always had to get the last word, gave me a serious look, and said: "Any American who walks the city of Baghdad will certainly be captured, and likely beheaded."

"That was not news from President Bush, it was American politics at its best. You guys picked up on it rather fast. Only a fool would attempt to do such a thing," Sergeant Todd said. I smiled, making no comments on the subject.

My Iraqi Logistics Officer, Major Salat made me aware of an incident that involved his uncle who worked for Saddam Hussein. "My uncle reached the rank of general and wanted to make changes to the Iraqi military. Saddam Hussein disagreed with any changes to his military. Saddam summoned my uncle to his office and had inhumane pain inflicted on him. Saddam's guards tortured his eyes by putting cigars out in them. After the treatment with the cigars, he was taken to the yard of the castle and shot in front of a crowd of ranking military officers."

While the major shared his story with me, a newly acquired interpreter to the team, nicknamed Spider, burst into tears and ran out of the room. Spider had previously told me that he was awfully ashamed of his country. "I do not want to leave my country. I want to stay here and do what I could do to help my country."

At the time, Spider truly believed that the Americans could help stop the violence. The others in the room, disagreed with

Spider, laughing at him, and calling him names. Including Major Salat. Then I asked the question to everyone in the room if they were better off that the American military was there?

"No!" They all yelled simultaneously.

There was a mixture of feelings about all foreign troops leaving Iraq since the fall of Saddam Hussein.

It all related back to the hanging of Hussein. Their feelings were that the Americans rushed to kill Saddam Hussein. As a result, many felt that led to an increase in violence all across the country. Many blamed the U.S. for their woes and wanted them out.

"Does that include Colonel Sam, Sergeant Tee, and me?" I asked. "Don't forget, we are American soldiers, and we would have to leave with the other Americans."

There was laughter in the room. One of the Iraqi soldiers said, "You are not an American soldier. You are from neighboring Kurdistan, and you are welcome to stay." I shook my head and begin laughing with the others.

"We are leaving, for sure, but no fixed date has been set," I told the group. Colonel Sam did confirm that our team would be the last to be airlifted out. He was also the same guy who had previously told me that we would be leaving a month earlier. Again, I was trying to deal with matters as they happened. There had been so many ups and downs during my tour. At that point, I was still learning not to get worked up over them.

I knew our time would come, and they could not hold us there forever. While we were having a conversation about leaving, news came down that ten coalition soldiers had been killed in a twenty-four-hour period by roadside bombs. The news was another reason for me not to become complacent.

"The American soldiers have been here four years already. We know Americans are dying, but what about the Iraqis?" Hani asked.

"That's a question I cannot answer. I understand your frustration." For many of the Iraqi soldiers and their families, it has been the hardest four years of their lives. They believed that their lives were better when Saddam ruled. Some shared how their life was before the invasion of Iraq. In their opinion, their families were better off and did not have to live under the daily threat of violence.

There was no way I could relate to their situation. Although, I did become a compassionate listener. I had spent nearly a year living among them. I saw the looks of despair on their faces almost daily. I had no idea what their families must have been going through while the soldiers were away.

I don't believe that many Americans soldiers or their families could have survived that ordeal. Few Americans are not even concerned about the circumstances of war, as long as the fighting remains abroad and we are winning.

Major Salat wanted me to know how hard the war was on him and his family. His daughter had been kidnapped once, and he paid a sizable amount of money to have her returned unharmed. Months later he was contemplating on moving his family to Sweden. He informed me during an earlier conversation that he'd earned his pilot's license in Sweden. Major Salat was afraid that something would happen to his family again. He worked on a plan for some time before sharing it with me.

"You are the only American who I told this story to. If you tell the other Iraqi soldiers about me, they will kill my family and me," the teary-eyed major said.

Listening to his disheartening story was hard to bear. I nodded my head several times acknowledging that I was listening, but I felt there was something strange about his story. True it was disheartening, but there was this senior Iraqi officer, whom I didn't know well, telling me this unfortunate story, and he was in tears. He wanted me to keep his story a secret. When I saw an opportunity to change the subject I did. I chose another topic to talk about, the weather.

We were entering the last week of April. Winter had passed, and the temperature was already climbing back up near the one-hundred-degree mark. When I mentioned this to Hani, he said, "living with the heat is part of life in Iraq."

The very next day, near the end of April around 0800 in the morning, there was a rare downpour of rain. It was a significant amount within a few moments. I was driving alone on my way to breakfast in the dining facility. I could no longer see the roadway. It was covered with water. Never in my life had I seen it rain so hard. The sky was almost as dark as night. When I finally arrived at the dining hall, I stopped the truck, jumped out, and made a mad dash, running for cover. A group of soldiers and civilian contractors were standing under shelter with their heads facing the heavens. I am not sure what they were thinking, but I felt that it was the end of times. One minute it was hot and sunny, and within a few moments, everything had changed.

Those were the very characteristics of Iraq. Things were forever changing and as a soldier there you had to change with the changes, including the weather. You adapted. My maturity was probably a factor in my ability to adapt. As a critical thinker, I evaluated most situations before acting on any. I was not questioning authority, but I wanted to ensure that following the orders given were lawful, and more importantly safe.

I would argue that the older one gets, the more difficult it becomes to keep up with the transformation of an ever-changing military. All throughout my tour decisions and changes were being made. Someone always thought that their way of doing business was better than the other guy. One bad idea I thought, was the extension of soldiers. There were units of soldiers on standby, waiting to come to Iraq. The Pentagon could have brought them over a few weeks earlier, instead of keeping soldiers that were burned out. Especially the infantry soldiers, who were constantly on patrols day in and day out. They were always on the move, chasing the bad guys, saving lives and doing it all in sweltering temperatures.

Their biggest joy was the day that they were to leave Iraq. For them to have to listen to the rhetoric, supposedly coming from top commanders that "the Army in Iraq is broken." was not pleasing to them. The Infantry soldiers were proud of the job that they performed. Yes, to some degree the Army was broken. The soldiers were dead tired. They exhausted themselves trying to fix a complex problem. They wanted to fix it and then go home.

It was then rumored that no unit would be withdrawing from Iraq until the military situation improved. At the time, no one knew for sure if the 'no-withdrawal' order was true or not. But I knew the idea was very unpopular, and unwelcomed. Soldiers hearing that we were going to have to stay longer in the land of chaos really let the air out of the balloon.

I knew nothing about how to win a war. But I didn't believe that extending the troops in Iraq would help win it either. Some of the soldiers were on their third and fourth tours, and still, the war wasn't close to being won. As the older soldiers use to say, "They had served their time in hell." Their time was up, and they should not have had to worry about leaving Iraq. Bringing in fresh troops at the time would have been the right thing to do. It may have not won the war, but it sure would have fixed the moral problems of the soldiers.

With only a few days left in April, matters deteriorated. Even with all the extra security forces that were sent into the heavily guarded fortress known as the International Zone (IZ), things did not look good. More NATO soldiers were dying, as a result of the rise in violence. Something had to be done.

As the number of days were getting shorter, another major catastrophe took place. Someone driving a truck bomb, was able to penetrate their way through the heavy security, killing several coalition soldiers in the Green Zone. But despite all evidence to the contrary, some politicians tried to spin that things were getting better on the ground. Despite their attempt to make things look good, it didn't work so well. The infantry soldiers knew the realities of the war.

The Iraqi soldiers who I was working with certainly differed with the assessment that things were getting better. I conducted my own survey among the Iraqi soldiers. Speaking through one of the interpreters, I wanted real people to give me their opinion of how things were going. They were in a better position to provide an accurate report of what was happening in their own neighborhoods.

Several Iraqi soldiers told me some of the most disturbing stories about violent acts that were carried out on innocent women and children in their neighborhood streets. Some of their stories were incredibly painful to listen to. My heart was filled with grief. I became like a sponge, soaking up their problems. At times, I felt as though I was a resilient American warrior, and other times I felt broken. My heart would ache whenever I would hear those misfortunate stories.

The security forces were building a wall around the city of Baghdad. I had mixed feelings about the wall. I saw putting up a wall as a divider of people, and not something that would bring them together.

I had to agree with Omar, when he said, "You know Sergeant Slade if Saddam Hussein had attempted to build a wall around the city, then for sure there would have been an international cry of outrage."

I thought the last thing needed in the Middle East was another wall. Within days of the announcement of a wall going up, there were scores of Iraqis protesting the matter. Protest over the wall generated opportunity for more violent attacks between the secular tribes of Iraq. There were many disagreements among the citizens in the city. But, most of them were united against building a wall.

An unknown spokesperson for the U.S. government, said, "It is not the desire of the US to separate people. It is the desire to control who goes in and out of the city."

I suppose I was getting more opinionated as I got closer to my last days. Some things became clearer than they were when I first arrived in Iraq. At the same time, I was more anxious as well. Being in the land of lawlessness, I had some thoughts over what could go wrong and disrupt my returning home.

There was still talk going around that the "brass" back in the Pentagon was working on a last-minute plan to extend some units. Given the fact that some soldiers had packed and shipped many of their essential items home, the news wasn't received well.

It was not easy after telling your family about your homecoming, and then just days before your arrival, you have to turn around and tell them that your stay has been extended. As we were approaching the last few weeks, the whole ordeal became more nerve-wracking, because nothing seemed confident.

A lot of chaotic developments unfolded in those last weeks. I witnessed American soldiers on patrol who were already stretched out thin and were stretched out even more, all throughout Iraq. Needless to say, everything was in disarray. There was an increased build-up of troops from the 82nd Airborne out of Fort Bragg NC, and Cavalry troops from Fort Hood, Texas. American assault missions increased on the radical militant fighters who had been launching relentless attacks against both NATO forces, and civilians. They sought to bring an end to the fierce attacks.

I was hoping that the lid would finally be put on the violence with so much fighting power on the ground. But I also thought about the loss of life, which were inevitable. There were nine paratroopers from Fort Bragg killed, and scores of Iraqi citizens during one major attack on the 24th of April 2007. It was said to be one of the worst days for the Americans in a year. On that day six Americans and five foreign troops were killed from the escalation of violence.

Days before my departure, I observed the capture of several insurgents just outside the wire. I saw several young Iraqi men, with their hands tied behind their backs, and their heads covered with dark green sandbags to prevent them from being able to see. They were being escorted off the military trucks and led into one of the medical facilities on Camp Taji. I suspected that some of the insurgents may have infiltrated the camp. It had to be a difficult job for security to distinguish between the contract workers and the insurgents. There were a large number of workers coming on and off the camp every day. Who's to say how many insurgents may have been able to penetrate their way inside?

I really got fidgety towards the end and did what I thought I had to do to survive the last few weeks of my tour. I kept a very low profile. Occasionally, other soldiers would speak about getting back home, and how they had grown tired of being in Iraq. Others didn't express themselves at all and bottled up all their feelings.

"Grown tired" was a fair way of summing up the feelings of many. I felt weary, as I got close to leaving, I remained vigilant, probably more than I was in the first few weeks. I prayed that nothing would go wrong.

18

Hearing the official news that we would be leaving was like being awoken from a bad dream. The mandatory extension issue was settled, and finally, it was decided that we would be added to the list of units returning to the states.

Our replacement unit had been in place for almost two weeks. In every aspect, they were prepared to take over all duties, except for those of my team. There was no replacement team scheduled to relieve Colonel Sam, Sergeant Todd, or myself. Colonel Sam submitted documents verifying that the Iraqi soldiers at the training school were up to par, well trained, and could take over for themselves.

The brigade along with my two team members were excited and ready to hand over all control and power to the Iraqis to make it official. Leaving was nothing like coming. Several soldiers in the unit got together and planned a beer bash. They wanted to have it in the noncommissioned officers club back at Fort McCoy on the night of our arrival. The beer bash plan triggered another morale fight. Not that I was a beer drinker, but I fully supported those who wished to organize the event. We were informed by a couple of higher-ranking noncommissioned officers, that orders had been issued by the post commander back at the home base that no alcohol would be served to returning soldiers from Iraq.

I was not able to confirm if it was true or not. Furthermore, it was difficult to determine the exact source of the military order, unless it was written in black and white. If it was a verbal order sent to the troops on the ground in Iraq, then it probably was twisted a lot before getting down to the soldiers.

To be frank, I wasn't sure why there was even an issue. The average age of the soldiers in the unit during that time was around 34 years old. That's considered to be years beyond a seasoned soldier. Given the maturity of most, many were baffled over a decision not permitting them to drink any alcohol upon returning to Fort McCoy.

Some of the soldiers were upset and declared to disobey the order if and when it was implemented into law. Why would adult men and women who just completed a major tour of duty in a war zone be denied the right to celebrate with a few beers? The majority of soldiers felt that each individual should be held accountable for their own conduct.

I assumed once the word got back to Fort McCoy informing the post commander how upset the guys were, it would probably be changed. If the order was legitimate, it's likely it would be challenged by the noncommissioned officers who were organizing the event.

Now that it was official and our time was running out, soldiers in the unit were rushing to complete last minute packing. They inventoried the last few items that needed to be mailed. Nervous energy was all throughout the camp for those of us who were scheduled to leave. At this point we were praying that nothing would go wrong.

Iraq was nowhere near being stable, and the war was by no means over. We were leaving the Iraqi troops in good shape, in terms of training and equipment. Once we were gone, several thousand NATO soldiers would be left back on the ground to carry out the combat mission. The situation in Iraq was worsening. Hardcore radical groups were attacking members of the Iraqi government, as well as intensifying their assaults on NATO service members. The U.S. government had spent billions of dollars preparing the Iraqi soldiers for those assaults, and it was fast becoming their fight to lose.

Hours before it was time to leave Iraq, I spent some time reflecting on both, changes and accomplishments, I had witnessed. I wondered if our coming there really did make a difference.

I knew my team members and I did our best to make improvements to a broken system. I worked closely with two professional soldiers and witnessed them pouring their hearts out, trying to make the Iraqis and the Iraqi army better. Both Colonel Sam and Sergeant Todd spent long hours each day working on either a project or individual assignments. And then there were times when all three of us would just sit and wait for the Iraqi soldiers, to agree to talk to one another. The Iraqi soldiers were well aware that the time would come when we would leave. With our departure, they would be forced to take full control of all their military responsibilities.

We had our setbacks, yet we were successful. We suffered no loss of life. However, two of our sister units lost a couple of soldiers due to IEDs. We spent long hot days and nights trying to fulfill our duties. There were differences among us all. Nevertheless, I am convinced that there were more agreements than disagreements.

In the end, the Iraqi soldiers seemed to figure out it was essential that they work together to succeed in their quest for peace. I credit many of the Iraqi soldiers I had the opportunity to work with for never giving up. We had many different view-points on how to move forward on a lot of issues. In the end we got there because we were finally able to agree.

Their style of leadership was clearly different from what I was accustomed to. When I thought the Iraqi soldiers were wasting time and doing nothing, they were actually in the middle of a period of thought. They were working things out without the involvement of outsiders.

No one could predict what the future in Iraq would be. I dare say that it was a better place when I departed than when I arrived. The war did nothing to halt sectarianism. There was still a divide among the Iraqi people, and we had no idea how successful their democratic government might be. There were obvious problems between the members of the ruling party. There was no unity, and neither was there trust among its members. The Iraqi government was fearful of being betrayed. Which grew out of corruption, and was believed by many to be a significant cause of death to many Iraqis. Trust was hard to obtain.

Like many others, I don't know the answer to peace in Iraq; however, I am sure that war will never be the solution that would bring peace to Iraq. According to research, the Iraqi military has been around since the early 1920's. The majority of the Iraqi soldiers that I came in contact with during my tour were not real warriors. My impression of them was that they were more of survivors. Their main goal seemed to be able to provide for themselves and their families. They also wanted peace, and return to a normal way of living.

In some ways, their goals were similar to my own, which was a peaceful solution to end the war, and a better future of my country. At the end of my Iraqi deployment, I made the decision to end, what was at times a challenging career. I put my personal life on hold, making the priorities of the army, my only priorities. It was a difficult time for both my family and me. We all made great sacrifices to meet the numerous challenges that we were confronted with. Being deployed to war was one of the most trying endeavors of my life.

19

The time had come. On our last morning, everyone was up early for breakfast and prepared for the final phase of processing out of Iraq. A little before sunset, a bus drove over to the west side of Camp Taji picking up Colonel Sam, Sergeant Todd, and myself. There were also a few other soldiers from a different unit who hopped along with us. We had been sitting outside waiting with our luggage, for most of the afternoon. The bus drove us a short distance from the barracks to a nearby staging area in an open field. We were reunited with other members in the unit; some of them we had not seen since we arrived in Iraq.

They had been on other missions throughout the country. It was a relief to see that they all survived and were safe. Everyone reminisced on their adventures of the past year while we waited to be picked up by two transport helicopters. We were scheduled to fly to Baghdad where we would spend our last night in Iraq, sleeping in tents at Camp Victory. That was to be our final staging area. On the eve of our departure the heat was very intense. I reached a point where I needed a break. My imagination ran wilder than usual, I sat on my stuffed duffle bag and stared up at the sky. I glanced at the sun and began to daydream. I watched the sun as it positioned itself to set behind the sand dunes far out in the desert. That was to be my last sunset in Iraq. One day I will reflect back and probably miss that large orange ball of fire. I felt like we had become well acquainted with one another.

That blazing Iraqi sun greeted me and followed me around in the desert each day. I know the sun is one and the same. However, that evening before sunset, that old desert sun appeared to be more massive and fiery than what I was used to seeing back home. On that particular evening, the sun took longer than usual to go down, it seemed; much slower than on evenings passed. Frankly, I believed that the sun deliberately hung around longer than usual, and took its time going down as its own way of saying goodbye. Its bright rays reflected off the dark tan dried out desert sand. As I watched my last sunset in the desert, it seemed all the natural surroundings were participating in the sun's grand finale.

Nightfall arrived, and a larger than usual full moon replaced the giant ball of fire. The stars even performed a glistening dance in the night sky. They were more visible and brighter than usual. I imagined they too came to say farewell.

When I arrived in Iraq, I was both terrified and lost. Taking my first steps on the grounds, I saw nothing that gave me hope. As I began my journey, my surroundings and also the sounds were very unpleasant. Nearly everything in my range of vision was unattractive.

The strong smell of oil burning from the pipelines filled the air, giving rise to large clouds of black smoke that hovered high up into the sky. The exploding of arsenals could be heard coming from almost every direction.

Now, as I was preparing to leave Camp Taji, the moon provided a bright light. I was able to survey the boundaries near me one last time. In spite of all its war ruins, I saw that most of the camp's natural features remained intact. This led me to believe one day, long after my departure, there would be hope for Iraq. I hoped that Iraq will be revitalized back to a healthy civilized society.

The soldiers got louder causing me to snap out of my stargazing and return back to reality. They were celebrating leaving Iraq in good spirits. Some of the guys were too excited to sit, so they ran around like children playing on a summer's eve.

Two hours passed before two large Chinook helicopters finally landed. Nearly two more hours passed, and we still were not cleared for takeoff. No one complained; all that mattered was that it was our final evening on the ground. We were leaving for good. The wait turned into a big party with lots of jubilant soldiers recounting their past year.

Not everyone on the grounds was celebrating, though. Rami, Hani, and Omar came to say their goodbyes with tears flowing down their faces watching as we prepared to leave them forever. I knew they wanted so much to go with us. We had become so attached to each other. We spent mostly twenty-four hours a day together during our deployment. We had become almost like family. It was difficult leaving them behind.

The three of them stood there heartbroken. We were the second group of Americans that they worked with who were abandoning them. We'd built a strong bond of unity with one another. I will forever miss each one of them. Colonel Sam, Sergeant Todd, and I owe 90% of our survival to Rami, Omar, and Hani.

They were our brothers. They had every right to say that the U.S. is indebted to them. America should have been obligated to help them by granting them a visa, to come to the U.S. It would have been a considerable acknowledgment for the work they did for our government. Especially for risking their lives, and the lives of their families, to help us. Many interpreters were working for the U.S., all across the country. Few received visas early on. Unfortunately, granting permits was not a part of what I or my team members did, they were granted by the State Department.

Moments before we were to board the helicopters, Rami cried out, "*Why, why, why*? Why is this happening again? Why, can't we go? Why are you leaving us behind?

I could not give Rami an answer, I could only give him a hug, which started the flow of my own tears.

The same questions that were being asked by Rami were the same questions that we had been discussing for some time. Why wasn't someone working harder to help them? The translators believed we would be their saviors and the ones who ensured they were granted good fortune and freedom. They trusted we would help them find a way out of their war-ruined homeland. After all, they went above and beyond to help us.

I had told them it was out of our hands. The visa was a sensitive issue. I prayed that someday, someone from the U.S. State Department or the Iraqi Minister of Foreign Affairs would help the three of them get a visa. They had already applied for permits ten months before our departure but received no response from anyone updating them on the process.

I felt that leaving them was almost like leaving my family all over again. It was like the very first time I deployed to Iraq. We had gotten just that close. When the call came to board the helicopters, it was bittersweet— everyone was infused with excitement, but, looking back and waving my *wadaeaan* (so long) to Rami, Hani, and Omar, was heartbreaking.

Their voices faded as the noisy engines of the helicopters roared louder. I waved and blew kisses. I thanked them for the time that they were in my life, and for their wisdom, which helped me to grow. Those three Iraqi men who I left standing there were my brothers.

The engines roared louder as the large Chinook helicopters lifted up into the night sky. Looking down I watched as the silhouettes of the Rami, Hani, and Omar faded away. So, did Camp Taji. I never heard from any of the interpreters again. There was part of me that felt insecure about on-going communications. I was fearful that my communications might be intercepted by the militants and cause harm to each of them, or to myself. We were told often in security briefings "not to get too close to the Iraqis." I still feel guilty about it. But, only the State Department could help the Iraqi people who put their lives on the line to help the U.S.

The physical part of my deployment had ended. It was the emotional part that remained with me. Being in that hostile environment was always a daily threat to life. Each day started normal, but as it progressed, something was forever happening. You could never bring yourself to totally relax. I was always on guard, trying to stay focused and safe. Most of the time, I attempted to withhold my feelings from others and tried to appear normal. On occasion, I wish I could forget the past and flush my memories down the drain.

When circumstances were too painful to bear, I could always count on a higher power to see me through. I continue to give thanks for my blessings up to this day.

I was torn over being a warrior, and a peacemaker. There was a part of me that just wanted to be human. I know my deployment was due to the choices I made, and I chose to serve my country. My experiences in Iraq proved that it was not easy. Regardless of the training I received, like many others, I deployed with a different attitude about the war, and I returned with an attitude different from the one I left with.

I learned a lot about the Iraqi people, their culture, and their views of the war. More importantly, I learned about their perspective on life. In the end, I departed with an understanding that they were just like many of the folks in my own community. They just wanted a simple and peaceful life, which meant serving their God, being happy, and providing for their family.

Both the Iraqi army and NATO forces were on the same mission. Both sides lost soldiers every day throughout the campaign to end the war. Some of the American soldiers boasted about winning the war. They made comments like, "we kicked butt today." It was good to hear that the soldiers on patrol were making progress, but I still was saddened to hear of the death of anyone being announced. Especially in terms of a celebration. Oh yeah, the celebration of "kicking butt" were on both sides. I guess that's one of the ultimate goals of war, go in and "Kick Butt."

When we boarded the plane in Kuwait for the last time, I was very emotional. I could hardly believe that we were taxiing down the runway taking off to go home. This time it was over, it was no dream. I prayed that we safely make it back to the States.

After hours and hours passed, and many miles far behind me, I started to feel more at ease. High above the pure white clouds and a distance from Iraq, I thought more about going home. I gave thanks to God that I was safe and I made it out that hostile environment in one piece.

The pilot completed all stops abroad and was finally preparing to land the plane at Bangor International Airport in Maine, on U.S. soil. He made an announcement welcoming us back home to the "Good old U.S. of A." As the plane bumped its wheels on the runway, every soldier on the flight yelled out in jubilation. My own scream was joyous as well. I tried to release all the emotional pain that I had been carrying since day one of the deployment.

Once the plane came to a halt at the airport terminal in Maine, everyone stood up, waiting for their turn to exit. Rushing through the gate at the airport, we paraded our way through an orchestrated crowd of senior greeters.

Some soldiers strutted around the airport like peacocks on tropical grounds. We were once again heroes to an aging population of American patriots.

I marched along on the coattails of the other soldiers, not wanting to look as if I wasn't proud of the accomplishments that we achieved as a group, it was that I never got used to all the attention that we were getting.

Nearby was a group of ladies with a couple of boxes full of refurbished cell phones. The cell phones had been donated by American citizens for the sole purpose of returning soldiers to call their loved ones. I walked by, and one on the ladies handed me a phone, who said: "Call your family, it's free."

What a beautiful gesture that was, to call home and to be able to say the words, 'I am home!' We were definitely back in America. It was the America that I was proud to serve. Not an America that was seen by some as mercenary invaders, or dividers.

Soon it was time to board the plane for our home base: Fort McCoy. This time we were flying across the great northern States of America. There was nothing hostile about flying there. Soldiers continued to sing, or exchanged humorous war stories about their recent adventures, causing laughter throughout the flight.

It was our final flight as a military unit. Never again would we fly as a unit, or a group of soldiers going off to war. That was it, we landed back at the same Air Force National Guard hangar where we'd departed from when we began our journey to Iraq.

We were back and unloaded the plane to be received as heroes for a final time. Standing by waiting were military commanders, all ranks of soldiers and civilians. The setting inside the terminal was a festive one.

The smell of fresh paint was lingering in the air. It was a bright yellow giving off a warm feeling of welcoming and not the usual dark army green which was used on most military buildings and vehicles.

There was a large stage erected with a massive American flag waving in the background. Patriotic music was being played as the generals, and other commanders took to the stage to make heroic speeches, giving praise for our return and accomplishments.

One-by-one every soldier marched across the stage, receiving an award for their bravery and sacrifices that they made while serving their country during a time of war.

When my name was called to march across that stage, I marched with a unique military stride, and nervously positioned myself in front of the commanding general to receive a folded US flag and a medal, in military tradition, for my service to my country.

At the end of the ceremony, everyone let out applause, along with shouts of "hoor...rah." The journey was officially over. From that point, everyone rushed to the waiting buses, taking us back to Fort McCoy.

The ride back to the fort took close to forty minutes. Approaching the main gate at Fort McCoy, were more cheers of excitement. We were back where we started. We were assigned to different barracks, in a different area, then when we arrived one year earlier. It was all open bay, and again no privacy. This time it did not matter.

Without unpacking anything, everyone just grabbed a change of clothes and took off like herds of wild animals. Everyone went in a different direction. Some walked, some rode the shuttle bus to the main post's shops.

I went along as well, not to shop, just to walk around and taste freedom without needing to have a weapon, and get a feel for normalcy. I stopped by the crowded internet café, were a long line had been formed as soldiers waited to send a message to their loved ones. I wanted to send a message to everyone I knew who'd sent prayers and thank them for their support, and their good wishes. I was out the entire evening wandering around the fort enjoying the freedom and walking around not being afraid.

As nightfall came, the whole group went to NCO club for the long-awaited beer bash. I did not drink beer, but I went because I wanted to spend a final evening with my comrades. It turned out to be a fun event. Most of the soldiers ordered their favorite dish. Some had steaks that overlapped their platters. Others chose plates that were utterly full of seafood.

I can assure you the post commander and the other commanding officials had to be proud of the way the soldiers conducted themselves. No one got out of line, and if they did, they were policed up by their battle buddy.

Our purpose for returning to Fort McCoy was to officially process out of active duty status and return to our reserve units. Which called for medical examinations, updating records, and to ensure things were adequately documented. The more significant procedures were conducted by the medical staff, who wanted to ensure everyone was physically and mentally okay.

The out-processing procedure took three days. After all the essential work was completed, we were released to return to our home states. We were bused to Milwaukee's main airport, where everyone said their final goodbyes to their comrades and battle buddies, most of whom we'd never meet again. That was a little emotional, but the thought of returning home eased those temperamental feelings.

Once inside of the terminal we were on our own. Everyone walked away in all different directions since we all were flying out to different regions of the U.S. I walked to my departing gate and eventually boarded the plane. This was a day I had dreamed about and anguished over, almost nightly for more than a year. It had finally become a reality.

When the pilot announced that we were landing in Greensboro, NC, I was ecstatic, and the happiest man on the plane. The other passengers must have sensed my feelings because they parted the way and allowed me to be the first to walk off the plane.

This time it was tears of joy as I rushed off the plane, down the walkway and saw my family members standing there, trying to withhold their own emotions. There were hugs and kisses, as we were reunited. I vowed to never leave them under the terms of war again.

However, it is essential that they and others know, despite my feelings for or against something, I always tried to respond with rationale and without judgment. Living in that chaotic environment had life-changing effects. I thought I already knew all about life, but being deployed taught me to be appreciative of the small things, and to give everyday blessings to the things I paid less attention to in the past.

I am no longer the man I was before deployment, I grew into the man that I am now. I experienced pain, hurt, loneliness, fear, and death. Those things were essential to me and my spiritual growth.

I came to see things differently and to understand that in life, some decisions are necessary. I am thankful for my great military career, and that I was able to serve my country.

Years have passed since my journey to Iraq, and at times I continue to struggle with that emotional deployment to war.

Acknowledgements

I must thank my wife of nearly 40-years for withstanding the great forces of pressure that were placed on her while I was away. Thanks to my son Jamie and my daughter Annika for staying strong, during a critical time when their lives were interrupted. Not only was I deployed, but emotionally, my wife and children were as well. I thank my parents and my family members for their support. I also would like to thank my late friend Heinz Ullrich, and my lifetime friend Cherita Isler for inspiring me to write this book. Thanks to the members of Locust Grove Baptist Church in Brown Summit North Carolina, and all my friends and family in Germany who supported me during that challenging period of my life. I also must thank Betsy Thorpe for her editorial work and helping to shape my manuscript. Thanks to the members of my memoir critique group who wholeheartedly transformed my writing.